GENDER SHOCK

Practicing Feminism
on Two Continents

Hester Eisenstein

BEACON PRESS   BOSTON

Beacon Press
25 Beacon Street
Boston, Massachusetts 02108-2892

Beacon Press books
are published under the auspices of
the Unitarian Universalist Association of Congregations.

98 97 96 95 94 93 92   8 7 6 5 4 3 2

Library of Congress Cataloging-in-Publication Data

Eisenstein, Hester.
    Gender shock: practicing feminism on two continents / Hester
Eisenstein.
        p.   cm.
    Includes bibliographical references (p.   ) and index.
    ISBN 0-8070-6762-8 (cloth)
    ISBN 0-8070-6763-6 (paper)
    1. Feminism—Australia.   2. Feminism—United States.   I. Title.
HQ1823.E47   1991
305.4′2′0973—dc20   91-16225
                                                                 CIP

Contents

Acknowledgments

For their help with the completion of this book, I want to thank Frances Goldin, my agent; John Iremonger, my former publisher at Allen & Unwin Australia (now Director of the University of Melbourne Press); my mother, Ruth Eisenstein; and Venetia Nelson for careful readings at various stages. I thank Alice Jardine for her contribution to the chapter on Harvard and New South Wales and Judith Stacey for her assistance in finalising the title. I am grateful to the Rockefeller Foundation for the award of a Changing Gender Roles in Post-Industrial Societies grant for 1989–90, which helped to support me during the revising of the manuscript, and which is underwriting my further study of the femocrats. (The Rockefeller Foundation is of course in no way responsible for the contents of the book.)

Although they did not contribute directly to the development of the manuscript, I am grateful to the American Studies Department, and to the Women's Studies Program within it, at the State University of New York at Buffalo, especially to Elizabeth Kennedy and to Michael Frisch, for providing me with a supportive atmosphere, both politically and intellectually, in which to think and work; and to R. W. (Bob) Connell, Kathleen Daly, Sondra Farganis, Martha Fineman, Lucinda M. Finley, Regina Graycar, Mari Matsuda, Isabel Marcus, Nancy K. Miller, the late Bobbye Ortiz, Rosalind Petchevsky, and Catharine R. Stimpson for a variety of kinds of intellectual and professional assistance during my simultaneous return to the United States and to academic life in 1988.

Finally, I am most grateful to my parents, Ruth and Myron Eisenstein, for their help during what seemed a parlous journey back to the United States; and to Michael Tanzer, my heartfelt thanks for seeing me through a long dark night of the soul into a renewed and shared optimism, despite the current difficult political climate. His support in many forms was crucial to the completion of this book.

Hester Eisenstein
New York
June 1990

Material from chapters 2 and 4 has appeared in print in slightly different form prior to publication in this volume, in:
'The Case for Feminist Optimism,' *Taking Issue: Grace Vaughan Memorial Lecture and Octagon Lectures, 1986*, Perth: University of Western Australia Extension, 1987;
'Femocrats, Official Feminism, and the Uses of Power: A Case Study of EEO Implementation in New South Wales, Australia,' *Yale Journal of Law and Feminism*, 2, 1 (Fall, 1989): 51–73; and
'Femocrats, Official Feminism, and the Uses of Power,' in Sophie Watson, ed., *Playing the State: Australian Feminist Interventions*, London: Verso, 1990, pp. 87–103.
The material is reprinted here with permission.
Chapter 6 is drawn from the 26 July 1986 broadcast of the Australian Broadcasting Corporation Radio National Series, *The Minders*, and is printed here with permission.

Part I

1 Introduction

In a kind review of my previous book *Contemporary Feminist Thought* Marian Sawer, an astute analyst of Australian politics, feminist and otherwise, suggested that the title of my next book might be *Contemporary Feminist Practice* (see Sawer, 1984). I have not quite taken her suggestion. But in fact the title I have selected does reflect the point of her remarks. Having done an account of the theory underlying the second wave of the women's movement (although only the United States version), it was perhaps time to focus attention on the practice and to ask some searching questions. What has feminism achieved, and where has it been frustrated? Have there been mistakes and false starts along the way? And, most crucially, what theoretical and strategic issues might we want to address for the coming decade (and century)?

In *Contemporary Feminist Thought*, I argued that feminist theory had reached an impasse in seeking to create a utopia of woman-centred values. It did not seem to me that this was a recipe for action in the real world. Yet it is clear that some of the actions inspired by a woman-centred utopian perspective have been palpable in their real world impact: I am thinking most particularly of women's role in the peace movement (see 'The Case for Feminist Optimism', page 82). Writing now, I find some of these distinctions more blurry than they had seemed at the time. But there is still, to me, a fundamental issue that remains unresolved for feminists, and that is how we get from the values we hold dear — of collective, non-hierarchical, democratic behaviour — to the outcome we seek, of a peaceful world safe for women and others now subject to discrimination, victimisation and oppression, without sacrificing these values in the rush to seize and use power on behalf of feminist ends. That this is not a new question in the world of politics does not make it any the more easily answered when raised from a feminist perspective.

3

In addition, this question needs to be placed in a different context now than when it was first raised at the outset of the second wave of the women's movement in the 1960s. We are living in an era in which feminist ideas and actions have had a major international impact. Feminist institutions and feminist interventions — from cultural productions and modes of political organising to the entry of feminists and other women into many traditionally male-dominated areas — have changed the intellectual, cultural and political landscape considerably, and perhaps irrevocably.

In thinking about this altered context, it occurred to me that what we are experiencing is something that could be called gender shock. (In coining this term, I am drawing on the general understanding and acceptance of the term 'future shock' as formulated in Alvin Toffler's widely read book; see Toffler, 1970.) By gender shock, I mean the shock that has been produced in society and in individuals by the successful introduction of feminist ideas. Gender shock can occur at many levels. It takes place, for example, in an audience that is being addressed for the first time by a woman speaking with authority. It occurs within a family when a woman imbued with feminist ideas begins to take her own needs and her aspirations seriously for the first time. It occurs within individuals of both sexes when they try to implement feminist principles in their everyday transactions, from the use of non-sexist language to the equalising of domestic or workplace tasks. And it occurs in institutions such as corporations, government agencies, and universities, when women begin to claim places at senior levels of the hierarchy.

In some ways the major moment of gender shock for our generation has passed: the 1970s and early 1980s saw an enormous cultural upheaval and the beginnings of a changed consciousness in many arenas about the roles of men and women. But in other ways it seems to me that the reverberations of feminist activism are only now beginning to be felt. One theme, then, of the essays collected here is the reception of feminist ideas in the culture at large.

Presumably some form of gender shock was to be expected from the general public. But perhaps we feminists, too, have our own version of gender shock. And here is where the issue of political strategy enters most crucially. How do we come to terms with some of the ways in which feminist ideas have been received, with all of the distortions, omissions and co-opting strategies that this has entailed? And how do we discuss these matters among ourselves, honestly and constructively, without having the feeling that we are washing our dirty linen in public (a form of women's work that is traditionally supposed to be carried out behind closed doors)? A second theme, then, is the struggle among feminists of differing persuasions to come to terms with the reception of feminism, which in turn raises a series of questions about coping with elements of success and with elements of disappointment or failure.

My own take on this set of issues has been profoundly influenced by an accident of my own biography. I migrated to Australia in 1980 and encountered a feminist culture that was at once familiar and deeply, at first incomprehensibly, different from the east coast United States feminist culture of which I had been a part. In particular, the creation in Australia of the category of 'femocrats' — feminist bureaucrats — and the political and cultural impact of these women on the Australian scene was, to me, an extraordinary achievement, and one that bore many lessons for the international debate about feminist interventions.

The result was a series of essays, written originally in a number of different contexts — lectures; academic papers; and a radio interview — in which I tried to come to terms with the ways in which my Australian experiences had reshaped my ideas about feminist theory and practice. The essays are printed here largely as they were written but with some revisions in order to turn papers and lectures into chapters. (Where information needed updating, this material generally appears in the notes at the end of the book.)

Part I of the book is introductory: chapter 2 recounts my experience of immersion in Australian culture and the consequences that this had for my thinking about feminism.

In Part II, I focus on the Australian debate over the role of the femocrats and the questions that this debate raises for the relationship of feminist activism to the state. Chapters 3 and 4 examine some of the issues raised about the politics of femocrats and their relation to the women's movement. Chapter 5 is a case study of Equal Employment Opportunity implementation in New South Wales, drawn from my experience as an affirmative action officer.

Part III is concerned with some issues raised by the successful reception of feminist ideas culturally and politically in the past twenty years. Chapter 6 is a dialogue between Alice Jardine and myself about the uses of postmodernist ideas for feminist theory, and about the experience of working as a feminist in the 'interstices' of male-dominated bureaucracies, whether in government or the academic world. Chapter 7 looks at optimism as a feminist political stance. Chapter 8 examines the concept of the family as analysed in feminist writings. And chapter 9 reviews some contemporary uses of 'gender' as a category of analysis within feminist scholarship.

I hope that this collection of essays and the comparative perspective they present between Australian and American brands of feminist practice will be illuminating to feminist scholars and activists, to social theorists generally, and to those — growing in number, I am sure — who consider that the effective implementation of feminist principles is one of the crucial ways in which the world can ensure its survival, in peace and equity, into the future.

2 Learning to speak Australian

In this chapter I want to begin the process of assimilating the experiences I had during eight years of living in Australia, experiences which I believe have marked me for life. I wrote *Contemporary Feminist Thought* largely while seated at the kitchen table of the temporary apartment provided to me and my then husband by the University of New South Wales. I began writing this chapter while seated in the study of my temporary lodging in Buffalo. There is, then, a quality of symmetry and closure to this exercise: I looked back at the United States and at the development of feminist theory there through an Australian lens, and I am now looking back at Australia and at the varieties of feminist practice there through a North American lens. The northern hemisphere foliage of Buffalo is deeply familiar to me from my childhood, but when I began writing this chapter, it still appeared somewhat foreign to me. So much had I immersed myself in the culture and environment of that extraordinary island continent which I first discovered in the pages of Henry Handel Richardson's *The Fortunes of Richard Mahoney*, borrowed from my father's library as a teenager.

Elizabeth Wynhausen, an Australian journalist and novelist who works in New York, remarked to me in 1987 that the only way I would find out what I really felt about Australia was to write about it. I have taken her words to heart. My experiences there were particular to a certain era now ended — that of the Labor Government of Neville Wran and then of Barrie Unsworth in New South Wales — and to a certain circle, that of Sydney femocrats and feminist scholars and their male allies and associates. I want, then, to capture what that era meant to me as a newcomer from the United States, moving from the world of the Women's Studies movement to the world of the femocrat — a change that had for me the quality of moving, as it were, from theory to practice, although to put it in these terms is to oversimplify vastly the meaning of both words.

6

When I moved to Australia, there were virtually no jobs on offer in academic life that suited my need to combine academic with feminist work. And so I took the advice of my new feminist friends in Sydney and entered the public service where I became a femocrat, that is, a feminist working in the bureaucracy for women's issues. The context of my work in Australia was that I was working as an affirmative action officer, first in the Office of the Director of Equal Opportunity in Public Employment (DEOPE) from 1980 to 1986 and then as the Leader of the Equal Employment Opportunity (EEO) Unit for the New South Wales Department of Education from 1986 to 1988. Hence it was part of my official duties to devise effective and persuasive ways to speak about feminism to audiences of senior public servants and other groups who were by no means inclined at the outset to be sympathetic. In some ways, coming from a background in Women's Studies where one was nearly always addressing an audience of the converted, this was refreshing, even bracing, in that one had to begin from square one and make plain one's fundamental assumptions so that these could be, if not embraced wholeheartedly, at least examined critically.

One of the features of Australian life that I found most appealing — and there were many of these — was the commitment to giving a fair hearing to people of an opposing point of view. I now believe that this has less to do with the presence of a lively parliamentary democratic tradition, although this was a powerful influence, than with a commitment to a concept of fair play in sporting events, which spilled over into all parts of life. I was astonished when I attended my first cricket game to hear the opposing team applauded as vigorously as the home team for displays of virtuosity. This was in strong contrast to my limited experience of American sport, for example at Mets games where it was *de rigueur* to boo opposing pitchers, batters and everyone else. This very English tradition seemed to carry over into the realm of ideas as well.

The respect for feminism and feminist activism, in the context of Australian culture, seemed in my mind to bring together two traditions: a long history of respect for, indeed, near-worship of, major female sporting figures — people like Evonne Goolagong Cawley, Betty Cuthbert and others — and the sport-influenced preparedness to give something new or someone new 'a go' or a 'fair go'. This was part as well of the dominant ideology of egalitarianism, much celebrated as the basis of Australian life (in contrast to the class-ridden society of the Old Country, England). Egalitarianism, of course, was more honoured in the breach than in the observance, given the class structure of Australia. And it had certainly never been applied to white women, as Anne Summers and other Australian feminist historians had made clear in their writings of the 1970s, nor to Aborigines, the original inhabitants, male or female.[1] But it seemed, as a system of beliefs, to influence the reception of feminist ideas once these became current and widely debated.

Feminism in the Australian context seemed to me, when I arrived there in the 1980s, to have been taken up culturally and politically in ways that were unfamiliar to me from my North American experience. On the one hand, there had presumably been nothing to compare with the vast and powerful media reception of feminist ideas at the popular level in the United States during the heady period of the 1970s, when the *New York Times* was taking it upon itself to explain consciousness-raising to the literate elite of New York. On the other hand, the political spectrum in Australia was profoundly different from that in the United States, and this had its effects upon the reception of feminism.

I remember reading the *Sydney Morning Herald* in my first few weeks in Sydney, and coming upon the use of the words 'feminism' and 'social-ism' as part of the daily vocabulary of the front page. This, when the *New York Times* was still strenuously resisting the use of 'Ms' to describe women like Bella Abzug (referring to her, comically, as Mrs Abzug). Some years before I moved to Australia I read a piece in the *Village Voice* by Pete Hamill where he had proposed that, to take the sting out of the word 'socialism' in the United States, we replace it by something more acceptable, say, 'stickball'. In Sydney, apparently, one could say both 'feminism' and 'socialism' without apologies.

The difference, I was to learn, had to do with the nature of the political parties and their ideological commitments. Unlike the United States Democratic Party, the Australian Labor Party contained within its ranks people who saw themselves as socialists, and the party as a whole called itself socialist, although the nuances of this escaped me when I first encountered the vocabulary of 'Oz' politics. But there was another point of difference as well, and this was the Australian willingness, even propensity, to call things by their correct names, to say out loud what as an American I was accustomed to saying in a whisper. Coming from a culture where I had believed that direct speech was part of my birth-right, I was astonished to have landed in a culture where the directness of speech made the Americans I had associated with seem mealy-mouthed.

It was not just in the discussion of politics that the directness of Australian language made itself felt. I found that people, men and women, had an affinity for all kinds of obscenities that I had never before encountered, and that the use of these was authorised in very public kinds of places. As someone to whom the right to use foul language had been part of my own coming-of-age, I was overjoyed. I soon learned the correct usage of words like 'ratshit', the meaning of which was fairly apparent, and other words, like 'drongo', which required translation (roughly, a dim-witted person, an idiot, perhaps derived from the tragic history of the racehorse, Drongo, who never won a single race; see Wilkes, 1978).

8

I also learned that directness of speech was part of a broader cultural pattern which replaced American hypocritical politeness with a kind of rough, confrontational style of discourse that, at first encounter, could be overwhelming. I am forever grateful to Jill Matthews, an Australian feminist historian who teaches at the Australian National University in Canberra, for tutoring me in the ways of Australian culture and, in particular, in the differences between Australian and American feminists. Early in my stay, Jill sat me down and gave me some lessons which she said would stand me in good stead if I wished to be well-received among the Oz sisterhood. American feminists, she explained to me, tended to be rather demonstrative and sentimental, especially in their California incarnation. (Her saying this saved me from taking offence as of course I could distance myself from the West Coast, being a card-carrying New Yorker.) In contrast, Australian feminists were fiercely unsentimental and would treat peers and others — especially newcomers — to a lot of sarcastic humour.

As an American I was very likely to be subjected to what was conventionally termed 'Yank-bashing', and people were going to 'take the piss' out of me (that is, mock me) for my accent, my American colloquialisms and my lack of local knowledge. If I was prepared to take this in good humour, I would be accepted readily. But if I bridled at it or took offence, I would be dead, finished, dismissed.

As soon as I encountered my first group of Australian feminists (from memory this was at a gathering held for me by the feminist sociologist and activist Eva Cox, whom I had met in New York before migrating to Sydney), Jill's warnings bore fruit. I was able to hear the rough humour aimed in my direction as a kind of a test of my flexibility, and to respond in kind. Events then unfolded as Jill had predicted: I was taken in and made part of an amazingly warm, vibrant and sophisticated throng of feminists, who were prepared to tutor me further in the ways of Australian culture, including extensive training in humour, language and drinking vast quantities of white wine. There is no telling what might have become of me had I not been warned ahead of time about how to behave.

As I began to know the Sydney feminists better, I was impressed by the breadth of their knowledge and the cosmopolitanism of their outlook. This was, I soon found out, a feature of Australian intellectual life about which Australians themselves were self-conscious. The 'tyranny of distance' (at least, from England and Europe as well as from the United States; Indonesia is a lot closer) forced Australians to look outward, and the 'cultural cringe' — only beginning to diminish in the 1970s and 1980s — reinforced this. For me the symbolic representation of this was the custom of one local radio news programme of following the announcement of weather for all Australian capital cities with a list of temperatures for some 20 foreign cities, alphabetically, from Ankara to

Warsaw. The Australians habitually looked out to sea, and to a larger world, partly to check themselves and their progress against other countries and partly to confirm their own uniqueness. In part, too, the migration to Australia of people from all parts of the globe following World War II reinforced this internationalism.

In the context of feminism, internationalism meant a full awareness of the work of writers from the rest of the feminist universe. I found that Australian feminists were conversant with the feminist literatures of the United States, England and France, as well as with other less obvious sources such as East and West Germany, Asia, Africa and Latin America. And the habit of international comparisons meant that they looked, for example, to Sweden and the other Scandinavian countries for models of social welfare programmes and other practices with relevance to the status of women. Having thought of myself as well-read in feminism, I was abashed to find myself rushing to catch up.

As a result of this international consciousness, Australian feminists had a kind of sophistication about theory and practice that I found very appealing. They were aware of, and respectful toward, the achievements of American feminism. But they were also prepared to be critical of its limitations and of its cultural specificities — something that until I had lived in Australia was not particularly in my consciousness.

An example of this is the debate over pornography that I attended some months after arriving in Sydney. The pro-sex/anti-s & m debate was just heating up in these years in the United States and the Sydney feminist community were eager to get an idea of what the Americans were on about.[2] At a specially convened meeting, a group of feminists watched a nonviolent but fairly steamy pornography film and then held a discussion about a feminist approach to pornographic material.

In the discussion, it became clear to me that the Sydney feminists considered that American feminists were reacting in part out of a nationally specific Puritanism toward sex and sexuality that they, the Australians, did not share. The influence of and respect for religious doctrines had nowhere near the emotional hold in Australia that they did in the United States, and of course there is not the history of flight from religious persecution that there is in the United States. And attitudes toward the body were very different in a country where topless bathing for women was commonplace on the beaches. Many Sydney feminists came out of a tradition of libertarianism, a strong cultural and political influence of the 1950s and 1960s, and had cut their political teeth on fights against state censorship. In addition, the already existing strict censorship laws tended to keep out of the country the worst examples of child pornography and violent pornography of the kind displayed in the slide show by the New York Women Against Pornography (for example, the magazine cover showing a woman being fed head-first into a meat grinder). The result was that the opposition to pornography lacked the passion and the conviction of the American anti-pornography campaigners. The flavour of the discussion, I recall, seemed to distance the Sydney feminist community from what its members saw as American feminist excesses on this subject. The anti-pornography campaign in Australia, from my observations, never had the bite and the widespread appeal of that in the United States.

A second example that stays in my memory was the visit of Mary Daly to Sydney.[3] Having heard Mary Daly speak in the United States, I was accustomed to the kind of reverence that she invariably received from audiences there. The Sydney audience took a different approach, asking her tough questions and raising difficult issues about the political implications of her philosophical views as expressed in *Gyn/Ecology* and *Pure Lust*. When Daly displayed a reluctance to defend her views, and indeed, in her responses indicated that she felt she had no need to defend them, the audience grew restive, and then openly challenging. The end result was explosive, with Daly losing her temper and with the audience responding in kind. I was shocked at the openness of conflict, but I was also fascinated. It seemed that the Sydney feminists were not prepared to take anything on faith. They were irreverent and sceptical, and expected their interlocutors — no matter how world-famous — to be prepared to defend a position in an eye-level kind of debate. This was a very different climate from the one I had become used to in the United States, where the fundamental egalitarianism of feminists could often be undermined by the 'star' system that gave certain speakers a privileged platform for their views.

By far the most significant difference between Australian and American feminism, though, was the degree to which Australian feminists had found their way into public positions of influence. 'The long march of feminists through the institutions', as Marian Sawer describes it, had created a unique network of feminists working within government, using 'a range of women's policy machinery and Government-subsidised women's services (delivered by women for women) ... unrivalled elsewhere'.[4]

When I arrived in Sydney, I was dazzled by the highly political feminists I encountered. They seemed utterly at ease with the structures of power at state and national levels. They understood the mysteries of bureaucratese, of applying for senior positions in government, of how to chair a meeting in order to control the outcome, of lobbying at endless, wine-soaked luncheons and dinner parties, and of the (to me, utterly impenetrable) rules of standing for preselection as a candidate for parliament.

These feminists were intensely practical-minded, and they were immersed, too, in a kind of detail that I found overwhelming and mystifying. I was to learn later that the initial training for this kind of politics was derived, in many cases, from a background in Irish Catholic family life where intrigue, mystery, the collection of useful private information about everyone who was anyone and a capacity for planning five or six moves ahead of your opponent seemed to have been imbibed with the holy wine of the sacraments.

These women, I was to find out, were mostly femocrats, a word of Australian coinage.[5] When I first heard the word, at the Anne Conlon Memorial Lecture of 1981, it was introduced to me as a term in common usage that often connoted a sellout or co-optation, as opposed to the true believers in overalls who inhabited the separatist communities of Glebe and Balmain in Sydney, where the true heart of feminist revolution lay. (My informant on all of this was Jozefa Sobski, herself a longstanding femocrat in the field of education and a respected activist in the New South Wales Teachers Federation.) The opposition, then, was between revolutionary feminism of the streets, outside the corrupt system of power and prestige, and the official feminism of the state, which created bureaucrats in its own images, painted birds whose role it was to contain and to dissipate the energy of feminism.[6]

According to Eva Cox's account, the decision to enter state and federal bureaucracies was a conscious feminist strategy, particularly among members of the main feminist lobby group, the Women's Electoral Lobby, after the defeat of the Federal Labor government in 1975 following the 'coup' (attributed in many circles to the activities of the CIA) that ousted the Prime Minister, Gough Whitlam. (The original femocrat was Elizabeth Reid, Whitlam's adviser on women's affairs, who was a political appointee rather than a public servant.) The purpose of this strategy was to influence policy through the state and federal public administrations, by means of the creation of women's units to develop legislation and budget allocations that would attend specifically to the interests of women.[7]

The strategy of creating a femocracy has gone hand in hand with a strategy of alliance with the Labor Party, which resulted in a strong voice for women in the Labor Government of New South Wales, and subsequently in the federal Labor government under Hawke, although at this writing the latter appears to be waning (a symptom of this is the resignation of Hawke's feminist Minister of Education, Susan M. Ryan, in 1988). In New South Wales, there were women's units in the Department of Industrial Relations, the Health Department and, most significantly, in the Premier's Department, with the responsibility, among other things, of preparing the so-called women's budget every year. This was a second go-round of the official budget process, whose results were announced on International Women's Day, with special allocations for women's programmes.[8]

Australian femocrats have become significant enough as a phenomenon for a literature to have grown up around them, debating all aspects including dress, behaviour and political commitment.[9] By the time I entered the New South Wales public service, femocrats had become a significant force for change. A whole generation of feminists had taken this route for a mixture of reasons including financial and professional ambitions, feminist and other political commitments, and blockage in other careers, most importantly, I believe, in the academic world, which had not — in strong contrast to the United States — created a world of Women's Studies to welcome, or at least to make some grudging room for, self-proclaimed feminist academics.

For me, what was striking about the femocrats was their undisguised commitment to feminism, and the acceptance of this within the bureaucracy. These were not a generation of women who, to win senior positions in government, had had to conform to the reigning ethos and disguise their personal convictions. Indeed, the demonstrated commitment to feminism had been, with some help from EEO programmes, incorporated into job descriptions. The spectacle of very traditional-looking male bureaucrats in pin-striped suits and conservative ties reading over the credentials of women candidates and discussing seriously their respective claims to authentic feminist commitment and political experience, is one that stays with me as a testimony to the effectiveness of the femocratic experiment, at least as a way into the ranks of the bureaucracy.

In getting used to the differences that I perceived between the women's movements in the United States and in Australia, an image kept recurring in my mind of the women's movement as a great river in flood. The river rises and then runs to the sea, and as it goes it moves into channels already carved into the landscape by previous floods. Of course it carves out some new channels, but it also runs most easily into the channels already existing, those places where it encounters the least resistance. As it shapes the landscape, the river in its turn is also shaped. I would not want to carry this metaphor too far (for example, what is the sea in this context?), but the image makes a point about the interaction between the energy and strength of the women's movement as a political and social force, and the political structures and social forms that it encounters.[10]

In the United States, one of the most visible and successful effects of the women's movement has been the growth of Women's Studies programmes. These have proliferated across the country and have continued to operate, if not to prosper, during the political backlash of the Reagan-Bush era. I do not mean to imply that Women's Studies programmes were established without a good deal of intense struggle. But in American universities and colleges there was a pre-existing structure available for adaptation, namely, the interdisciplinary curricular programme. The prototypes of American Studies dating from the 1950s, and of Black Studies introduced in the 1960s, presented a ready model for the new Women's Studies curricular offering. Particularly in the less traditional universities such as the University of Michigan and the University of Wisconsin, Women's Studies readily gained a foothold. From these pioneering places it spread to such bastions of conservative academic life as Princeton, Yale, Dartmouth and Harvard. The pre-existing channels for the women's movement in this case were the interdisciplinary curricular offerings and, more broadly, the tradition of innovative curricula as a social change model within the traditions of American education.

In contrast, Australian academic life is more austere and traditional. Interdisciplinary offerings have tended to be regarded with suspicion, and university curricula tend to remain divided along the boundaries of the traditional disciplines of history, politics, philosophy, economics and the like. The exception to the rule would be the newer and more experimental universities such as La Trobe in Melbourne, Macquarie in Sydney and Griffith in Brisbane. But overall, Women's Studies has had a much more difficult time making its way into the legitimate curriculum, although there are signs that this situation is now beginning to change. A similar resistance to the introduction of Women's Studies may be seen in colleges of advanced education whose curricula have been geared to more vocational and professional areas such as teacher education, nursing, business studies and technical education. During my years in Australia there was nothing that could compete with the expansion and legitimacy of Women's Studies courses, the range of Women's Studies academic positions and the flood of publications that characterised the field in the United States.[11]

The pre-existing channel cut into the Australian landscape, therefore, was not the world of academe, but rather the bureaucracy. Entry into the public service in state and commonwealth government has, as noted, been the target of choice for feminist activists since the period of the Labor Government of Gough Whitlam in 1972–75. Despite the controversy, the trend of creating femocrat positions continued unabated and is now a phenomenon that fundamentally shapes the women's movement in Australia, for better or for worse. Femocrats are rife, directing the Office of the Status of Women in Canberra, and women's advisory units, equal opportunity offices and anti-discrimination boards, particularly in state governments where Labor is in power.[12] While the debate continues over the status of the femocrat, and many in the women's movement may still see these as traitors to, rather than representatives of, feminism, there is no doubt that 'official feminism' (as I have begun to term it) is the most visible public product of the women's movement in Australia.

No doubt in focusing upon these two channels in the United States and Australia I am neglecting a thousand other areas where the river of the women's movement has changed the landscape. But I select these two in part because of the impact I believe that they have had in helping to shape the concerns and the expression of feminist theory in the two countries. It would, I believe, be hard to overestimate the importance of the Women's Studies phenomenon in shaping feminist theory in the United States. Similarly, the femocrats and their absorption into the state apparatus are now, and will increasingly become, the focus of a debate about women, the women's movement and the state in Australia.

This experience of contrast, then, is what shaped the writing of the essays in this book. As I became absorbed into the world of the femocrats, and the Australian feminist movement more generally, I learned not only a new language (I now claim to be bilingual in American and Australian), but I acquired new perspectives on feminist theory and practice from my immersion in the very political world of Sydney in the 1980s. Only some of what I learned appears in these essays but I hope they reflect some of the cosmopolitanism and the passion, the deep conflicts, but also the inspiring political commitment of the 'refractory girls' who were my mates and colleagues in those years.[13]

Part II

3 Feminism and femocrats

The starting point for this chapter was the curious 'fantasies and falla-cies' incident of March 1985. I had been invited to speak at a national conference on women in post-secondary (higher) education, convened by the Federation of Australian University Staff Associations (FAUSA, a national trade union for Australian academics). Several days before the convening of the conference, and no doubt aimed to coincide with it, a scathing critique of 'feminism's fantasies and fallacies' by Professor Leonie Kramer was published in the *Sydney Morning Herald*, 28 March 1985.

Professor Kramer, at that time Professor of English at the University of Sydney and former head of the Australian Broadcasting Corporation, often traded on her considerable reputation for scholarship in English and Australian literature to rehearse anti-feminist arguments from a fam-iliar vantage point: that of someone who claims to have needed and received no help from feminism, feminists or women altogether in her rise to senior academic standing. On this occasion she launched a fierce attack on affirmative action (AA) and equal employment opportunity policies. She upbraided feminist bureaucrats and academics alike for an alleged 'obsession' with counting and numbers, and for their insistence that women might have some claim to equal representation with men, in universities and elsewhere in society.[1]

I used the occasion of the FAUSA conference to defend what I saw as the legitimacy of using EEO and AA programmes for the advancement of academic and administrative staff women. I was seeking to refute what I took to be Kramer's criticisms of such programmes as an attack on feminism itself, broadly defined.[2] Needless to say, mine was not the

This chapter is based on a paper presented at the Australian Women's Studies Conference at the University of Sydney, 20–22 September 1985.

only response to Kramer's broadside. What was interesting for the purpose of my argument here was that other answers evoked by the Kramer piece defended feminism on quite different grounds. They took the view that Kramer was mistaken to think that feminism overlapped with AA and EEO, or even that they were at all linked to one another. One refutation sorted Professor Kramer out as follows:

> What is outlined as feminism's preoccupations in the article is known more popularly as equal employment opportunity or affirmative action which is the Australian variation of an American management theory. This theory selectively appropriates feminist critique to develop programmes to achieve change in the distribution of workers in the workforce in certain areas without necessarily altering its fundamental bases. It uses quantitative and some qualitative measures for evaluating change. Feminists are divided as to its efficacy and ambivalent about its practice.[3]

I found this a curious conjuncture. In fending off an attack from the anti-feminist right (in female form), some feminists were saying, yes, EEO and AA are part of feminism and we should defend both. But others were saying, no, feminism is not to be confused with AA and EEO programmes, and we should defend the one but not necessarily the other. It struck me that within this contradiction lay a series of unspoken assumptions, and that these were playing themselves out inside as well as outside of the academy. I thought therefore that it might be worthwhile to attempt to tease out some of these assumptions and to raise some questions about them. More broadly, it struck me that the argument was implicitly, if not explicitly, an argument about feminist interventions into the 'system' and about the critique from the vantage point of the women's movement about some of the reforms that have taken place in Australia since 1972 as a political response to the organised women's movement.

In raising such an issue, I was of course not particularly an innovator. The issues surrounding the legitimacy and the effectiveness of feminist reforms and of the proper attitude of women's movement activists toward the practitioners of 'official feminism' is a familiar debate on Australian soil. It has come up at the national Women and Labour conferences as a regular feature, and it was on the programmes of the Australian and New Zealand Association for the Advancement of Science (ANZAAS) conferences for two years running in 1984 and 1985.

This debate has struck me as curious but not unfamiliar. The controversy over the Australian phenomenon of the femocrat, when I first encountered it, was reminiscent in flavour to a set of arguments that had been going on for some time in New York. Women's Studies academics in the circles in which I travelled displayed a similar antagonism — a 'more feminist than thou' aloofness — toward the affirmative action and equity in education programmes mounted by state and federal governments in the United States. These were seen as reformist, as insufficiently radical and, ultimately, as co-opting both in their purposes and in their outcomes. I say this in the full knowledge of having participated myself in this attitude and having propagated it to my students and colleagues. We all enjoyed the sense of moral superiority conferred by the conviction that while affirmative action-style reformers were tinkering with the system at the edges, what we (Women's Studies teachers and students) were engaged in was truly radical and world-changing.

The debate seems particularly curious in the current climate. In Great Britain, our sisters have commissioned a book expressly in order to explain to British readers how it is that Australian women have managed to create such a remarkable degree of access by feminists to the state apparatus (See Watson, 1990). In the United States, my former colleagues ask me in amazement how Australian women have managed to win national affirmative action legislation during the same historical moment in which the Reagan administration was doing its level best to dismantle affirmative action in the United States. Australian feminists, meanwhile, have been spilling ink to demonstrate that EEO and AA legislation are capitalist snares and/or gifthorses whose teeth would have borne closer inspection prior to purchase.[4]

I think it is important to take a close look at this reaction. Is it a form of the Australian cultural cringe? Is it part of the 'tall poppies' syndrome (analogous to the American habit of 'trashing'), a reaction within the Australian egalitarian ethos to those who have become too famous and too powerful? Or is it, indeed, a genuine, serious and reasoned assessment of the power of the state to co-opt and to control women's energies and, specifically, the energies and commitments of feminists? In raising these issues, I allude to two sets of phenomena. One is the fact of the existence in Australia of a form of official feminism, as part of the policy of Labor governments, state and commonwealth. The advent of Labor governments has meant the proliferation of femocrat appointments: to women's advisory councils, women's units, to EEO offices and others. The second is the negative reaction to the growth of official feminism by feminists, some inside and some outside the bureaucracy, and most notably in the academy. The reactions range from reasoned critiques[5] to sarcastic off-the-cuff responses like calling the Prime Minister's office for women's affairs 'the Office for the Women of Status'[6], or indeed, the invention and use of the term femocrat itself, although the pejorative connotation of this seems to have faded somewhat over time.

There are several ways in which the debate over the femocracy can become a fruitful source for further feminist theory and practice, rather than continue as the slanging match it has tended to become in recent years. First, it seems to me that we need a data-based analysis of the phenomenon of official feminism so that one can talk about the measurable impact of the reforms under way. Instead of pronouncing upon the character of official feminisms, national and international, from some preconceived theoretical position about the inevitability of patriarchy (or whatever), we ought to be studying it from a variety of points of view. What do we consider to be the achievements of official feminism? What are its failures and limitations? And against what standard is it reasonable to take these measurements?

Secondly, and growing out of this research, it seems to me that there is a need for a more sophisticated discussion of the role of the state in legitimating feminist discourse and issues and in directing and controlling feminist energies — a contradiction that bears further examination. Having established an inventory of the reforms that we judge to have grown, directly or indirectly, out of the political pressure brought to bear on the state by the women's movement, we need reasoned discussion of the effects of these reforms, both on the status of women and on the character of the women's movement. Some of the categories of reforms to be looked at would be the impact of women's refuges and domestic violence legislation; the effects of reforms to laws on rape; the effects of the introduction of AA and EEO legislation; the impact of providing (and cutting) funds for childcare; the outcome of campaigns for equal pay, and for equal pay for work of comparable value; the effects of legal reforms on the freedom of homosexuals and lesbians; and changes to legislative and judicial regulations on abortion, on birth control and on pornography.

Thirdly, there is a need for a renewed and intensified discussion of the objectives of feminist action in the future. In an account of the impact of feminist reforms in Australia since 1972, Eva Cox points out that in the 1970s there was a concerted effort among Australian feminists to enter the bureaucracy as a conscious strategy for the achievement of feminist objectives. This strategy, in her view, was all too successful, creating 'a new mandarin class of women whose livelihood depends on the proposals put up by the women's movement'. Cox is sarcastic about

> the new American model corporate feminist who seems to encompass all those things I once loathed about women, together with much that I loathed about men.

Yet Cox concedes that the outcomes she is describing bear 'the marks of success, an idea in its time, taken on by the state and incorporated by the structure'.[7] Her point is that what the women's movement had in mind when it set out was a transformation, a major social change, in which the outcome was a significant redistribution of income and power. What it got, instead, was a small share in the spoils of power for a few carefully selected women.

Some femocrats take exception to being characterised as mandarins, although the phenomenon to which Eva Cox is alluding is certainly recognisable. We indeed wonder if we are deluded in exempting ourselves and our friends from the general description.[8] My point here is, however, that Cox and other observers concede that the outcome of the political struggle of the women's movement has been, among other things, the creation of forms of official access for women's issues and concerns. The question remains, how is this apparatus being used? And what use can be made of it by the women's movement?

Australian feminists have been vocal in their sarcastic dismissal of visiting North American purveyors of corporate feminism. Evangelical feminists of the stamp of Sharon Lord, EEO consultant and former adviser to the Pentagon, preaching the gospel of assertiveness training and dressing for success, have not been well received. Their advice has been dismissed, along with the notion that pushing women higher and higher on the corporate ladder is in any way advancing the goals of feminism as a radical social movement.[9] Yet my feeling is that a kneejerk reaction on this keeps us from looking more closely at the implications of winning access for women to positions with high salaries. I am speaking here less of women in business (although I wonder if we want to stand in their way) than I am of women who rise to positions of influence in the public service bureaucracy where they are in a position to develop policy.

It is true that these positions pick up only a tiny percentage of women, and that these women are not likely to be drawn from the ranks of those who are impoverished, and deprived of education.[10] Nor are they likely (unless the job is specifically designated as a specialist position) to be drawn from the population of Aboriginal women or women of non-English-speaking background, whose needs are the most urgent. But in my view it remains significant to have established the principle that women are no longer excluded from aspiring to senior positions which carry with them high salaries, power and influence. After all, overcoming the overwhelming poverty of women is a major feminist objective.

In addition, women's access to policymaking makes it likely, although not certain, that women's working conditions can be improved. Femocrats are in a position to bring to the attention of senior policymakers the centrality of such issues as maternity leave, equal pay, childcare, sexual harassment and women's educational and training needs. The access of women to policymaking positions in trade unions is particularly crucial in this regard. That so-called women's issues have begun to find a place on the agenda of legitimate industrial issues, is directly the result of the entry of women into senior trade union positions. The attention now being paid to the issue of repetitive strain injury (RSI) is only one of many examples here.[11]

In all of this it is crucial to begin to develop some historical perspective on our contemporary women's movement. I am arguing here for the need to do more sociology and more political economy of the women's movement itself. The femocracy is the most visible outcome in Australia. But one could look at many other areas where feminism has built new institutions, or altered old ones. For all of these, a historical and political self-consciousness about the dialectic between the women's movement and the social and political institutions of the countries in which it is active is crucial, I think, for any discussion both of achievements and of future objectives.

Finally, I think it is important for feminists to take account of what has been built in the past couple of decades. However limited and precarious the achievement, these are the structures that we have been able to construct so far. I think that achievements like the creation of the femocrats in Australia and the success of the Women's Studies movement in the United States require us to reassess our views on power and powerlessness. There is an old, familiar train of thought growing out of the counterculture of the 1960s that still shapes our thinking. This contrasts collective decisionmaking and egalitarianism which we see as part of the values of feminism, with bureaucratic structures built on hierarchy where decisionmaking comes from the top down. We extol the one and condemn the other.

Is this framework sufficient for our thinking in a time when, as feminists, we have started to enter and to shape some of the hierarchies? We know from the insights of Jo Freeman that power in collective structures can operate more invisibly than in a hierarchy, and can be more cruel.[12] It strikes me as a fantasy that the operation of power in an academic department, even in a Women's Studies programme, escapes the bureaucratic imperatives of competition, posturing, lying and other forms of gamespersonship. What then is our current vision for the empowerment of women, and what is our current experience? I say all of this not because I pretend to have answers to the questions but, on the contrary, to urge that we begin to pose and repose some of these questions in a manner that can interrogate our actual lived experience rather than our hopes and wishes.

Among Australian feminists there is a sense that, as between femocrats and practitioners of Women's Studies, the latter is a more legitimate enterprise than the former because it (Women's Studies) is less subsidised. It is precarious and starving and thus, somehow, more honest. Femocrats, in contrast, are numerous and well-paid. Therefore there is something rotten about them. The argument implicitly seems to be that Women's Studies is *a priori* more subversive than femocracy because it has been kept marginal. Yet the reverse argument would apply in the United States, where government action, at least at the federal level, is seeking to dismantle social programmes of all kinds, while

Women's Studies has become sufficiently institutionalised, generally, to resist such efforts. The danger to Women's Studies in the United States is that it is losing its subversive quality and has become respectable. As Ann Snitow as written,

> feminist scholars had better look to their style of communication and to the professionalization of feminist inquiry or fall short of an ancestry full of descriptively rich, polemically daring, and evocative prose — not so much quoted in feminist research, one suspects, so that the new scholarship on women won't sound too radically different from the old, which presumably never gushed, digressed, or shed a tear.[13]

The stance of 'more radical than thou' among different brands of feminists keeps us, among other things, from assessing correctly the strategic importance of feminist intervention in the state apparatus. We should not be misled by superficial indicators of status. Women's advisers may be well paid but they are also struggling in the bureaucratic hierarchy. Presence is not the same as access, and access is not the same as influence. We need to have some detailed accounts of the struggles behind closed doors. In addition, I would argue that rather than seeing the high salaries of femocrats as a sign of co-optation and cop-out, we should see these as a measure of the success of the women's movement while at the same time being prepared to use this success as a lever for further change.

Obviously this further progress depends, as has been noted many times, on dialogue and interaction between femocrats and the women's movement as a whole. As Jean Baker Miller notes in the United States context,

> if feminism is encouraging women to enter institutions, then it has an obligation to nourish a criticism of those institutions so that women can act to change them.[14]

But all of this depends on having a foothold or a toehold in the institutions in the first place. At a minimum, the establishment of femocrats acts as a buffer against the backlash, creating, as Miriam Dixson has written, a

> small but socially significant minority crucial to feminism's social base ... [providing an] enduring base for continuing social discourse on the meaning of gender ... .[15]

At a maximum, femocrats can use the ideology of the state against itself, performing a kind of feminist judo to bring reforms into being. Historically the state in Australia has acted paradoxically as an agent for the interests of capitalism, as a brake on the power of capitalism and as a defender of the interests of labor (although this was traditionally defined as the male working class). In seeking to use the state as an engine of reform, feminists are thus in a respectable tradition. The issue now is getting beyond tokenism, in the strength we wield, and looking more closely at what it is that we seek to achieve. If we do now have some stake in the institutions of power, however precarious and minimal, what are we seeking to use it for?

Apropos of the French women's movement, Francoise Ducrocq has written along similar lines.

> The old ways of struggle are not always the worst: to lay siege to the strongholds of male power by taking up positions on, among other things, the need for a real emancipation of women through economic autonomy, to establish systems of provisional alliances, to weigh on the weak links of the chain, to push the egalitarian logic of the socialist ideal so that women also benefit by it, is perhaps less thrilling than to stand aloof in a radical integrity. But some of us do estimate that it is the only effective tactic.[16]

If the dialogue on the question of objectives has not yet commenced, then I believe it must start now. As feminists we can no longer pretend that we have had no impact. The contemporary women's movement has raised the consciousness and the aspirations of women around the globe. And it has begun to make the voices of women heard, both culturally and politically. To scorn this achievement is to disempower ourselves and to risk stagnation.

4 Women, the state and your complexion

The problematic of this chapter is the search for a useful framework for discussing feminist initiatives that make use of the state apparatus. In the past few years an international debate has arisen about women and the state in the context of the apparent success of feminism in enlisting the use of legislation and of bureaucratic offices of various kinds in aid of feminist and feminist-inspired social reforms. Catharine MacKinnon has argued that for all of its theorising contemporary feminism has no proper theory of the state.[1] Yet internationally feminists are making use of the state, of governments — local, state and federal — and, in turn, governments and political parties are making use of feminism and feminists. What kind of alliance is this? What are its implications? What frame of reference is appropriate and meaningful to make sense — in the Australian context — of the 'femocrats' who are the most visible category of women embodying (and profiting from) the alliance with the state?[2]

By way of placing the title of this chapter and my thinking on these questions in context: some years ago I served on the planning committee for a conference at Barnard College (Columbia University) in New York. Funded by the National Urban Studies Association, the objective of the conference was to bring together the two interdisciplinary fields of Urban Studies and Women's Studies in some sensible fashion. This was a project that perhaps had more to do with the imperatives of academic expansionism than with a straightforward intellectual inquiry. In any case, the title selected for the conference was 'Sex, Gender and the City'.[3]

While the planning was going forward, an April Fool's issue of the

This chapter was originally delivered as a paper to the Sociology Association of Australia and New Zealand Annual Conference at the University of New South Wales, Sydney, on 14 July 1987.

Barnard student newspaper appeared with a special article on the forth-coming conference. The headline read, 'Sex, Gender, the City, and Your Complexion'. This piece of well-aimed satire has remained in my mind as emblematic of the dangers and pitfalls of the entry of feminism into academic life which has, as mentioned, its own imperatives. But it also took on a larger meaning, and that had to do with the ambiguities and complexities of contemporary feminism, with all of the consequences, intended and unintended, of the global reception of feminist ideas in the past couple of decades.

Many writers have remarked upon the capacity of contemporary hegemonic culture to co-opt feminism, and to spit it back at us in myriad ways that we feminists — earnest in our attempts at achieving profound and lasting change — greet with despair and anger. To illus-trate this, one can cite the 1987 advertising campaign from the perfume house of Chanel: 'Coco — un nouvel parfum, pour une nouvelle femme' (Coco — a new perfume, for a new woman). The new woman — with echoes of Gabrielle ('Coco') Chanel herself, a new woman of the 1920s — gets the same old commercial treatment. Yet even in the most commercial-seeming manifestations, the impact of feminism is complex, multilevelled and not insignificant. It is in the context of the reception of feminism at a number of levels — cultural, social and political — that I want to raise some questions about the Australian femocrats, as a case study of a new woman. I provide questions rather than answers, as it seems difficult to grasp the significance of so complex, global and fast-moving a phenomenon as the international women's movement.

Can feminism itself give some guidance in analysing the impact of the women's movement? That is, does feminist theory provide a framework for understanding feminist practice? One way into this problem is sug-gested by Nancy Hartsock in her discussion of the concept of a woman's standpoint.[4] By this Hartsock means the perspective that women, as women, have upon the world, which she sees as a privileged epistemo-logical vantage point, an Archimedean point of leverage from which to understand and to change society.[5] Hartsock argues that women (on the model of Marx's vision of the working class), by virtue of their experi-ence, have a universalistic *prise* (grasp) upon reality. This enables them to see, and to express, a certain set of truths that are obscured from those in a culturally and politically hegemonic position.

Hartsock makes, perhaps, too large a claim. But her analysis does have some merit, in my view, based as it is on the experience of consciousness-raising as the chief epistemological tool of the contem-porary feminist movement. The truths of the second wave do, indeed, stem from the tradition of 'speaking bitterness' by women. The question I would pose here is, what use can we make of this tradition in trying to get a grasp on what the phenomenon of the femocrats means? The question takes on some urgency in the current political climate. At the end of the twentieth century, the issues raised by the second wave, a global log of claims for women, remain as an ongoing list of demands which at the time of writing have not been met. There is a widespread feeling of despair, or at least of disillusionment, among feminist activists, who grow weary of repeating *ad nauseum* (although perhaps to ever broader audiences) what it was, exactly, that the women's movement was seeking to achieve.

This is not, however, to imply that the issues raised by feminism have gone unremarked. At least in Western countries, a large number of changes have occurred which can be traced, at least in part, to feminist activism.[6] Even to claim that these changes are due to feminism and its impact, rather than to forces governing changes for example in labour market activity, is considered contentious in some circles. The difficulties of proving anything about historical change in a manner that would satisfy the strict test of some social scientific approaches are notorious.

But without quibbling too much about cause and effect, one can nonetheless say that first, in the 1960s and thereafter, the women's movement revived internationally, and produced activism, cultural production and a series of demands for the betterment of women's condition in a number of countries. Second, initiatives have been taken at a number of levels by governments and international organisations that bear at least the label of women's interests and concerns. The varieties of official state feminism include the United Nations-sponsored conferences marking the International Decade for Women in Mexico City, Copenhagen and Nairobi, the establishment of agencies taking women's issues as their central concern (such as women's units and ministries), and the passage of legislation designed to embody the interests of women via changes to the legal framework governing marriage, rape, child abuse, domestic violence, sexuality and women's economic interests, encompassing both social welfare policy and employment issues such as equal pay.

Spurred on by the big chill of Thatcherism and Reaganism (and at this writing Greinerism in New South Wales), many feminists and other analysts concerned with social process and social change are trying to get a handle on what all of this activity has meant. Lynne Segal, in her complex and troubled account of the women's movement in Great Britain, has raised some hard questions about what the movement has achieved and where it is heading.[7] In undertaking any such analysis, it is critical to have some sense of the meaning of official feminism. The contradictions in this debate are striking. In her *Signs* articles, Catharine MacKinnon appeared to be ruling out any possible role for law and the state in furthering the interests of women because of the irredeemably patriarchal character of law and democratic government. Yet it was MacKinnon who, along with Andrea Dworkin, initiated the use of anti-discrimination law in the United States to establish the principle that pornography represented an attack upon the civil rights of women.[8] The gap between theory and practice here surely requires attention.

What then of the femocrats? Gillian Calvert has provided a working definition of the femocrat as

> a public servant who is feminist and is perceived to have control over either policy or funding or both. The fact that femocrats often do not really have that power is the source of friction with the women's movement at large, which is disappointed when femocrats fail to effect the sort of changes it would like.[9]

Calvert goes on to explain that

> people outside the public service use the term to describe any female public servant working in the area of women's policy, but feminist public servants are more likely to point to the women at the top — the heads of women's units and the women's advisers ... If one of the main aims of feminism is to effect fundamental social change, then femocrats are prime movers. Through lobbying, submission writing, representation on government committees, policy making and community education, femocrats help to ensure women's needs are taken into consideration in many spheres of government that affect them, including housing, education, health, social security and employment.[10]

The article on femocrats is illustrated with a self-mocking portrait of the femocrat at her desk, complete with notes on proper appearance: hair ('conservative, but can be gelled up'); jewellery, cut of clothing, shoes, briefcase, and other required accesssories. Shades of Lesley Lynch's beige suits![11] The self-consciousness about the femocratic uniform speaks volumes about the ambiguities of the role. And Calvert's definition, too, is filled with ambivalence: the women's movement thinks we are more powerful than we are. But we are influential: indeed, we meet the objectives of the women's movement through our actions. (Translation: the women's movement should stop being mad at us: for being too powerful; for being insufficiently powerful.) The phenomenon of the Australian femocrat simply cries out for a sophisticated analysis of a kind that has not yet been forthcoming in feminist journals or elsewhere.[12]

In developing such an analysis, the first point to note is that the term femocrat now covers a variety of types of officers. For example, in the array of feminist bureaucrats in the state administrations of New South Wales and South Australia, there are significant differences as to their locations and functions.[13] There are differences too, within New South Wales, between femocrats who are EEO officers (implementing Part IXA of the Anti-Discrimination Act) with responsibilities in affirmative action on behalf of women, Aborigines, migrants of non-English-speaking background and persons with physical disabilities, and femocrats whose brief it is to defend the interests of women only. And there are differences, too, between women in the bureaucracy whose brief it is to talk about and to prepare policy proposals concerning women's interests, and women who are identified as feminists only as a matter of personal conviction but not as part of their official work. These latter women may engage in significantly feminist behaviour within their organisations (lending support to other women, for example), but themselves seek to direct their careers within the so-called mainstream. This requires taking on roles that involve line management and that have a significant impact upon the distribution of financial and other resources for the organisation as a whole.

That femocrats of the former kind cannot by definition be seen to have a mainstream role is itself emblematic of one of the structural constraints upon feminists in the bureaucracy. For years in the Premier's Department of New South Wales it was common parlance to refer to the Anti-Discrimination Board and the Office of the Director of Equal Opportunity in Public Employment as 'satellite' agencies, that is, outside of the mainstream, along with the Art Gallery of New South Wales, as opposed to the Cabinet officers and others carrying on what was perceived as the real business of government.

All of these categories of officers are in some sense femocrats, that is, feminist bureaucrats. But there are significant differences among them, not least of these being the degree to which each would identify herself publicly as a feminist or would be so identified by her colleagues and by others in the system. More specifically, they would vary as to those who were and were not considered to be feminists in an official capacity, that is someone whose feminism was considered a qualification by which she was selected to carry out the duties of the position she occupies. That feminist sympathies and commitments of the kind that can be documented in a resume have come to be considered a bona fide job qualification in state and federal bureaucracies is one of the more remarkable achievements of the Australian women's movement.

A second point worth noting is that the femocrats now engage in a variety of tasks within the bureaucracy, and these are distinguished by the differences in content of the policy work. Any study of the significance of the impact of femocratic work would have to take account of these differences. For example, femocratic interventions in the area of social welfare issues have quite a different character from those in the area of affirmative action, the variations having to do with political alliances, the history of policy formation, the relevant legislation (or lack of it) and other elements in the development of the office in question. In short, the work of femocrats has become specialised and differentiated to the degree that individual case studies would be required to make any kind of accurate assessment of their actual impact on policy.

Thirdly, it is important to find for the analysis of the phenomenon of femocracy a framework that will encompass it in all of its diversity. Some writers have taken the view that the existence of femocrats is simply an instance of co-optation by the state of the energies of the women's movement. In this interpretation, a traditional Marxist perspective on the bourgeois state meshes nicely with the concept of patriarchy in the works of Mary Daly, who sees such women as 'painted birds'.[14] But I would prefer to see the femocrat phenomenon linked, somehow, to more contemporary Marxist views of the state as a terrain of struggle, where political and economic interests vie for power and influence.[15]

When I first began my work as an EEO adviser in New South Wales, I had the task of explaining the concept of discrimination to audiences of public servants. Often one of the only ways 'in' to a discussion of the issue that was accessible and relevant was to evoke the experience of some veteran public servants in an earlier generation of the struggles between Catholics and Protestants for control of various agencies within the public service. More recently, a senior woman bureaucrat in Canberra reported to me a conversation making this same analogy. In this instance she was addressed in her (putative) capacity as a representative of all women in the bureaucracy, present and future, and was asked mockingly, 'Well, what will you women have?' Without missing a beat she replied, 'We will take Treasury, Finance and Prime Minister's, thank you very much!'[16] Is the influx of feminists into the bureaucracy in the same category as the battles of yore between members of religious groups? Are femocrats simply a previously excluded outgroup now seeking access like other waves before them, on the model of generations of immigrants? Or are there significant political, economic and cultural differences created by the access of women and, specifically, of feminists?

One of the difficulties in developing such an analysis is the tension between practitioners in the bureaucracy and academic analysts. There has been something of a gap in perceptions, vocabulary and assumptions between these two groups, namely, feminist academics and femocrats. When I mentioned this article to a femocrat colleague her reaction was one of impatience: 'I am sick of that debate! We are just getting on with the job.' Among femocrats, the angst and self-doubt of some years back has been replaced with a sense of achievement or, to borrow an expression from the boys, of getting runs on the board. There is a sense of having made a difference. Femocrats have, for example, seen concrete improvements to the conditions of service for female employees, achieved through intervention by women with access to male decision makers (for an account of one such shortlived achievement see 'The Uses of Power'). This has weighed in the balance against the sense of being exploited or used by the bureaucracy. If a femocrat asks herself the question, 'Am I a highly paid bureaucrat who is in place to thwart or delay social change?' (like the characters in 'Yes, Minister'), the answer has to be no. This is often in stark contrast to men in parallel positions on similar levels of salary. These blokes are in fact concrete representatives of patriarchy, in some instances, and the task of the femocrats is to outmanoeuvre them, to beat them at their own game, as it were, by ensuring rather than preventing action on a particular set of issues.

The feminist located in the arena of seeking to use state power on behalf of women, perforce finds herself within a framework of liberalism or social democracy. One is taking the rhetoric of the liberal democratic state at its word, and stretching it to cover women as bourgeois individuals. Here the framework suggested by Zillah Eisenstein makes sense: the political tradition of liberalism excluded women until recently. In stretching it to include women, the concept of bourgeois individualism is challenged because women are not only individuals but members of a sex-class, a gender, with interests that are collective.[17] Thus there is room to manoeuvre within the structure of the welfare state.

But some academic analysts of state power tend to turn up their noses at this kind of a framework. Some are immersing themselves in a poststructuralist world view where the achievements of feminism have no meaning because the terrain of political struggle has been abandoned for the terrain of discourse. Others insist upon either a rigidly old-fashioned Marxist analysis of the state that leaves no room for the concept of conflict between interests within the state, or on a radical feminist vision (in the post-Daly sense) that discounts any achievement as ipso facto meaningless because it has occurred within the framework of patriarchal structures. Any of these modes of analysis, it seems to me, will wind up dictating the outcome rather than actually taking account of the lived reality of the struggle that is taking place at a number of significant levels.

The data base for the material I am presenting here is my own experience in the New South Wales state EEO programme, so this should be borne in mind in considering the comments I have to make. There is enough material for another chapter (or book) to give a full account of the EEO programme, its achievements, and the many critiques levelled against it in a number of fora.[18] The programme was instituted under Part IXA of the Anti-Discrimination Act as amended in 1980, with the central agency implementing the programme established in September 1981. So the programme has a history in New South Wales of some nine years of operation.

The EEO amendment has its roots not only in feminist activism, but in the simultaneous reform and modernisation of the public service in New South Wales under the aegis of the representative bureaucracy concept of Peter Wilenski, whose review of the New South Wales Government Administration led directly to the introduction of the Anti-Discrimination Act of 1976 and thereafter to the 1980 affirmative action amendment.[19] In introducing the legislation, Wilenski and his colleagues were trying to meld together two things: efficiency and equity. As a footnote on the outcome of this effort one should consider the work being carried out on current directions being taken in the public sector, especially in the Commonwealth, which ditch equity summarily and which conflate efficiency with massive restructuring and amalgamations, resulting in increases in the managerial tier on the one hand, and in part-time work on the other.[20]

The impact of the EEO legislation is highly visible in the number of senior jobs held by women, the changes to personnel practices and procedures, in a general familiarisation with feminist concepts, and in the use of feminism as a job qualification. There have been significant increases in representation in state government of Aborigines, migrants, and (much less successfully) people with physical disabilities.[21] The attitudinal differences are marked if one compares the public with the private sector where affirmative action is only just now painfully making its way.

Of course I may be painting too rosy a picture here, as someone who has been directly involved in implementing the EEO programme. In the measurement of impact, the statistics produced by the responsible central agency might be suspect on the ground of interest. It could be argued that there is a need for independent research on this. There is also a suspicion in some quarters that EEO at the top has been matched by a whittling away of the public sector at the bottom: a reduction in jobs; and the transfer of resources from the public to the private sector via the contracting out of some functions. During the period of implementation of the EEO legislation, there has been a history of cross-over and clash with traditional trade union concerns: for example over the introduction of internal grievance procedures, which were hotly contested by the New South Wales Labor Council as usurping for management a traditional role of trade unions. (This issue was eventually resolved via negotiations involving the Labor Council, the Director of Equal Opportunity in Public Employment and the Public Service Board.) Yet one can argue that many of the work issues particular to women and/or migrants and Aborigines were never taken up by the public sector unions until the EEO push forced the issue. Some examples here would be sexual harassment and racial harassment. On the other hand some issues have been less successfully pursued by the EEO initiative, notably public sector child care.

What kind of a reform, then, is this? And more specifically, what has been the role of femocrats in this process? The model that has developed in my mind is one of feminism finding niches and cracks in the system, and making its way in. EEO is not strictly speaking only about women. In New South Wales it has been part of a reform that overall shifted power from the Public Service Board to the Premier's Department, and it is also related to moves by government to cut across the power of trade unions to control public sector decision making. EEO thus has made some feminists into curious bedfellows with management. But nonetheless women have found their way in, and women's issues thus have found some significant public legitimacy.

It should be noted that the structure of the reform being introduced is highly bureaucratic in style. EEO requires annual reports which are statistically based. This means that improvement is measured in numbers: counting increases in the recruitment of target groups; counting budget allocations on staff development regarding EEO issues; and looking for other examples of measurable change such as the number of women serving on selection committees, the number of people attending selection techniques training and the like. It is, then, a reform shaped in the mould of the service it is seeking to transform. Hence it is acceptable in its language and it is readily drawn into the bureaucratic culture it attempts to remodel. Critics are inclined to ask, how radical a reform is this? The answer I would give is, not very; this is why it has been accepted.

But there are all kinds of other outcomes that are less easy to measure statistically. And this is the point where I return to the issue of women, the state and 'your complexion'. It seems to me that one such hard-to-measure outcome is that there has been a certain contestation of the masculinist character of the state. The influx of senior women who are self-consciously in an alternative mode has subtly altered the atmosphere (as opposed to the high numbers of women in subordinate positions who do not shift the balance of power). Here one can cite what might seem to be trivial incidents: a woman putting lip gloss on during the deliberations of a selection committee for a senior officer; a colleague stopping work to show off the new outfit she has bought at a sale (an incident self-consciously prolonged by a colleague of mine who said that usually the only thing that her fellow officers did during a coffee break was discuss football endlessly); a member of a women's unit taking the time to cuddle someone's baby in core time. What does this mean? Is it without significance? If not, what is the significance?

There has certainly been a certain infusion of ideas about women, power and sexuality. This is the inevitable result, for example, of the introduction of a sexual harassment policy, especially if it is vigorously implemented. How is this experienced? In an organisation such as the Department of Education, having a Grievance Officer who is a committed feminist and activist (such as Doris Owens, a long-time member of the Teachers Federation and a brilliantly talented negotiator, whose presence in the Department of Education during the period I served there — from 1986 to 1988 — left me with a vivid impression of the difference one person can actually make), and giving rank and file women teachers access to her, means a palpable shift in the power they wield in their own classroom. This changes the terms of debate in the bureaucracy. Let me not exaggerate: the actual power wielded by femocrats is well and truly limited, just as it would be, I imagine, for any influx of a new kind of person not previously allowed into the decision-making levels of the bureaucracy.

Another important question is, what happens to the women themselves? How do they experience their acculturation into the bureaucracy? This needs to be talked about; they need to be interviewed about the before and after. What are their experiences of mentoring; of learning the ropes; and of the roles they have to step into and/or develop in order to achieve the minimal level of acceptance necessary to operate with any impact at all? What quasi-kinship structures are being developed here? Father/daughter? Mother/daughter? Sister/sister? Brother/sister?

Within the women's movement, Chloe Mason has developed the terms 'big sister' and 'little sister' to talk about the generation gap that has emerged between the senior bureaucratic feminist — she who can write a funding submission in her sleep — and the new feminists who are coming up as a second or third generation. This emerged at the Women's Electoral Lobby 1986 conference in Canberra to consider items for the National Agenda for Women, where the expertise of the big sisters was juxtaposed with the energy, enthusiasm and radicalism of the little sisters, sometimes resulting in angry exchanges.

This dynamic was particularly in evidence in the debate over future strategy on equal pay. In the wake of the decision by the Arbitration Commission not to take up the issue of comparable worth, that is, equal pay for work of comparable value, on the ground that this formulation reflected the American campaign on this issue but not the history of arbitration decisions and the structure of wage fixation in the Australian context, Edna Ryan argued for the need to respect the decision and to find another way of putting the case forward. But some of the little sisters expressed outrage, saying, in effect, don't you counsel us to give in to the patriarchal constraints of the Arbitration Commission! We are going to use the term comparable worth anyway.[22] Within this debate one could perceive at least two kinds of struggles, one over defining the actual issue and a second over the use of feminist experience and tactical *nous* or know-how by younger and less experienced activists. Similar kinds of struggles go on among femocrats in the bureaucracy all of the time, although these are less visible and public.

Then there is the related question of the networks of women within the bureaucracy and how they interact with one another. How does the solidarity of women come unstuck when confronted with the pull of institutional loyalty and identification? Is one foremost a feminist, committed to the international struggle of women for their rights, or is one a servant of the Crown? An example of this is how little material I can actually use from my daily experience in the Department of Education, without jeopardising my own position! But it goes deeper than that: tests of loyalty are imposed upon femocrats daily. In addition, they are drawn into complicated strategies — expectations that we will leak certain information to certain networks in order to achieve certain outcomes . . . very much in the manner that, for example, an industrial relations officer can use contacts with trade unions to effect a certain set of manoeuvres that lead to a negotiated settlement of one kind or another in an award or an arbitration agreement. In short, the feminist 'mafia' is strong enough to have links inside and outside government agencies in the manner of many other such blocks, although this is still precarious compared, say, to the power of the trade unions.

What about the issues raised by Clare Burton about masculinity protection and the influx of feminists — and women, generally — into the patriarchal enclave of the workplace?[23] Burton argues that including women in the workforce at senior levels is threatening to men who have learned to define their own masculinity as deriving from inhabiting a space where 'women's' concerns — especially babies and children, but presumably also fashion and make-up — are definitively banned. Are there visible effects here?

Finally, and most crucially, there is the issue of whether femocrats are making a difference. The presence of women at senior levels seems to go hand in hand with the defence of women's interests. It is as crude as this. But how do we define these? In her analysis, Suzanne Franzway concentrates upon the welfare state and women's economic dependence.[24] But this narrows unduly the field of what women's issues are seen as encompassing. The debate over this continues: how does the state construct official feminism, if I can put it like this? A perfect case study here would be the the second 'bite of the cherry' in the budget process provided by the Premier's International Women's Day Speech every year, where women's projects get special extra funding. Is this window-dressing, or is it a form of redistribution?

There are issues, too, about language and style. The minute we start talking about the State, it seems to me, we fall into the trap of sounding very male/patriarchal. Consider the language I have been using here. Where is the space for women's culture in all of this? The women in the bureaucracy regularly get into trouble for behaviour that is too 'womanly' — that is, extravagant, emotional. (This of course is not only a women's issue. Juliet Richter tells the story of having a cup of coffee with an Italian male colleague, and having a perfectly calm and peaceful exchange interrupted by a solicitous colleague at the Public Service Board who rushed over to put an end to what he thought was a heated argument. It turned out that the conversation had been accompanied by a lot of hand gestures, and this was what had caused the alarm.) As a result, some of us deliberately monitor our language, and gestures. I am raising here a point both about the language we use to describe the femocratic phenomenon and about the language used by femocrats themselves in finding a path through the bureaucracy. One has only to take a look at the beautiful rich colours of the Women's Advisory Council newsletter and compare its appearance to the sober blue and white appearance of the Public Service Notices. It seems like an astonishing influx of life, diversity and colour into the drabness of pre-feminist public service life. But does this matter?

I do not wish to underestimate the degree of difficulty that carrying out this level of analysis would entail. I am aware that some aspects of the kind of study I am calling for here participate in what may seem to be the unspeakable and the unsayable. For example, one would need to address the sexual politics of the bureaucracy. In discussion with colleagues, I have had interesting conversations about the curious phenomenon of feminists lobbying and influencing male decision-makers and the kind of relationships that develop in this context. This raises, again, my point about quasi-kinship relations. There is a strong alliance of femocrats with sympathetic progressive male bureaucrats and extending, on occasion, to political figures like cabinet ministers and Members of Parliament. These relationships take on a quality of . . . how to describe it? . . . conspiratorial mateship across the sex barrier. There are nuances here as well. Heterosexual women perforce have a different style in this to lesbian women. This again needs to be dichotomised, into lesbians known to be such publicly, and those remaining in the closet for palpable and sensible reasons of career and basic personal security. While these matters are hard to discuss, they form part of the fabric and need to be studied.

Among the thorniest of issues in the phenomenon of the femocrat is that of conflict between women. The need for analysis of this appears to be obvious, yet the barriers in the way of carrying it forward are enormous. There is an overwhelming reluctance among most feminists to be involved, or even to appear to be involved, in what is in effect the 'washing of dirty linen' in public. There are too many actors on the scene (male *and* female, I am constrained to say) with an interest in exploiting conflicts among women. Femocrats are well aware of the need for presenting a united front in the press and in public more generally. But why is it impossible for us to find a way of discussing the sometimes terrible and searing conflicts that have arisen? Are these conflicts among women more terrible than those taking place all of the time and very publicly indeed among men? We certainly discuss our own conflicts 'privately' *ad nauseum*, and I believe that we are deluding ourselves if we think our male colleagues — past masters at sniffing out and making use of conflicts — are unaware of them.

In addition, the existence of conflicts stems sometimes from the most legitimate of sources. The differences in perception, in style, in tactics, in negotiating manner and in political views among femocrats are significant. In many cases these differences are totally explained by the location of the person, her objectives and her convictions on a given matter, shaped often by personal experience. It is almost as if there were a reluctance to admit the possibility that women, and indeed feminists, might have as wide a range of views of the world as would a similarly located group of men. We would be better served if differences could be examined so that we had a better sense of how they arose, in what structural contexts they erupted and then — oh, unattainable ideal — if we could find ways to mediate them and restore solidarity.

I conclude then with the point I raised at the beginning about women's experience as the basis of feminist knowledge. As feminists in the bureaucracy, we need to begin to speak — and when necessary, to 'speak bitterness' (the Chinese revolutionary practice which was one of the sources of the feminist tradition of consciousness-raising) — about our experience. To academic inquirers, feminists and others, I say, give us femocrats a break. Talk to us! Interview us! Let us get onto the historical record with the lived experience of the women at the coal-face of the bureaucracy. When I was visiting Rice University in Houston in April 1987, I asked a feminist academic there about the current state of play on the debate over pornography, which has divided the feminist world in the United States into two camps, known as the pro-sex and the anti-s & m factions respectively. What is the latest?, I said. What are people saying? The reply was, Look, everyone is keeping silent.

I found this shocking, and thought, We must not let this happen to us. I cannot bear the prospect that, having once broken our silence as women, we find then that we are in a situation where we are silencing ourselves — and our sisters — in the name of feminism. We need to find a way to record, analyse and debate the experience of femocrats in a way that gives due weight to the complexity of the phenomenon and the world-historical significance which, with all due modesty, I believe it has.

5 The uses of power: a case study of Equal Employment Opportunity implementation

The theme of women and power is one that has been a constant element in feminist theory since the resurgence of the women's movement in the 1960s. In this chapter I hope to contribute to this ongoing discussion, using as my primary source material my own experience in Australia in the world of the femocrats. The methodology I employ is a form of participant-observation, writing contemporary history from within in a mode given the stamp of approval by Staughton Lynd some years back but which I carry out with some trepidation nonetheless. The method of using one's own experience to build theory has a solid basis within feminism to be sure — what else was consciousness-raising about? Yet in the current academic climate of epistemological relativism, which gives the empirical, let alone the experiential, short shrift as a path to knowledge and truth (indeed, using these words already condemns me as a hopeless clinger to universalising thought), I feel, well, uneasy.

I will return in my conclusion to this question of feminist methodology for theory-building. I see this undertaking as part of a larger enterprise, being carried out internationally, to assess the impact of a wide variety of feminist interventions.[1] Since the 1960s, feminists have been part of a number of activities seeking to realise feminist goals, using whatever structures and resources they could find at hand. If one were to construct a preliminary categorisation of feminist interventions, it might look as follows.

Category 1. *Bureaucratic-individual*: entering the bureaucracy of state

This chapter was originally delivered at the Feminism and Legal Theory Conference, 'Women and Power', held at the University of Wisconsin–Madison Law School 27 June–2 July 1988. A shorter version appears in Sophie Watson (1990), pp. 87–103, and in the *Yale Journal of Law and Feminism*, 2, 1 (Fall 1989), pp. 51–73.

or national government at a policymaking level as a self-identified feminist.

Category 2. *Bureaucratic-structural:* creating new structures within government or university administrations to benefit women (for example, women's policy units; Women's Studies programmes; Ministries for Women's Affairs).

Category 3. *Legal reform:* introducing new legislation, or revising existing legislation to benefit women (for example, anti-discrimination laws; changes to the law governing rape).

Category 4. *Political participation in a leadership role:* running for some form of political office (broadly defined) as a self-proclaimed feminist (for example, the Ferraro vice-presidential candidacy in America; seeking to become a mayor, or member of a legislature; seeking to run for office in a union).

Category 5. *Alternative structures:* creating a feminist organisation outside of the mainstream of existing political and administrative structures (for example, women's refuges or rape crisis centres).

It is a matter for debate among feminists, inside and outside of the academy, as to whether any of these interventions has really improved the status of women. It is particularly difficult to assess some of the activities that partake of what I call official feminism, actions that involve state participation in women's affairs or women's concerns, as these are variously characterised by governments and bodies such as the United Nations.

Yet I believe that some assessment is required at this historical moment in which the politics of feminist commitment has such a crucial role to play on the world stage. In seeking to make such an assessment (and the above list of types of interventions is by no means exhaustive), a number of variables must be taken into account. The set of variables most vivid to me, given my recent experience, is the significance of national differences in shaping feminist interventions. The history I am presenting as a case study makes sense in the context of Australian feminism. How relevant is this to other places?

It seems to me that national differences are in fact important in shaping feminist interventions, and that they have at least three components. First, there are the national political differences between any two countries. I mean this in a pre-feminist or patriarchal sense, looking at the political culture of the country without, for the moment, looking at its indigenous feminisms. For example, an important difference between the United States and Australia is the difference in the role of unions in the two countries.[2] In Australia, the workforce is more than 50 per cent unionised. The powerful unions and their national organisation, the Australian Council of Trade Unions (ACTU), have an important voice in state and federal politics, particularly under a Labor government. In sharp contrast, in the United States union membership has dropped to below 20 per cent and the influence of organised labour has waned significantly in the Reagan-Bush years.

Second, there are national differences in the character of the women's movements, as these have been shaped by — or perhaps more accurately, as these have developed in the context of — each country's political structures. Thus, to continue the example, the campaign for equal pay for work of comparable value has a different configuration in Australia than in the United States because the structure that determines salaries and wages is completely different. Australia operates under a centralised industrial arbitration system, while the United States has a decentralised collective bargaining system.

Finally, there is the particular mix of feminist theory with practice that has emerged in each country. At least some of the differences of the kind that I observed in comparing Australian to American feminism stem from the national character (to invoke a much discredited term) of the feminist theories most current in a given culture, and the effect of this upon the explicit and implicit objectives of local feminist activity.[3]

Australian feminists appear to me to operate on the basis of a socialist-feminist praxis linked to the politics of the welfare state. This gives rise to campaigns and objectives that centre upon the protection of the economic rights of women as workers and as mothers, whether or not they work outside of the home. Thus feminists have focused upon issues such as welfare rights; child support payments; protection of women through extending union coverage (for example, in the garment industry for work done at home); and so on. In contrast, American feminists working in the area of legal reform are in many instances drawing upon the tradition of radical feminism, with its basis in gender theory, and concentrating on the debate over equality versus difference. This gives rise to campaigns and objectives that centre upon the extension of legal rights to women as a 'sex-class', for example, in the campaign to characterise pornography as sex-based discrimination.[4]

To generalise in this way is obviously to falsify the situation somewhat. All strands of feminist theory are present both in the United States and in Australia, and there is overlap in the range of activities and commitments connected to all of these strands. But the point I want to make here is that it is crucial to observe the interaction between local feminisms, in all of their varieties, and the structures of power within which they are compelled to operate. For feminists seeking to assess the impact of feminist interventions, it is very important to see clearly what strands of feminist theory and practice are picked up by and articulated into the structures of power, and what are the implications of this process for the ultimate outcomes. In the longer run, the shape of feminist victories and defeats will be determined by this dialectical process.

I turn now to the raw material of my experience as a femocrat. By the

1980s there were sufficient numbers of femocrats, at least in New South Wales, to be divided into specialisations. In addition to health, child care, welfare, legal reform and education femocrats, there were also femocrats edging their way into very 'male' areas such as the Treasury and the Water Board. And there were people like myself, who were Equal Employment Opportunity (hereafter EEO) femocrats, whose job it was to make sure that more and more women — among other groups — followed their sisters into positions of significant influence.

The EEO legislation in New South Wales was introduced in September 1980, as an amendment, Part IXA, to the Anti-Discrimination Act of 1977. The legislation established the Office of the Director of Equal Opportunity in Public Employment as a body to oversee the implementation of the law, and required all authorities scheduled under the amendment to produce an Equal Employment Opportunity Management Plan, which was to be submitted to the Director for her approval. The Plan was to be statistically based and was to establish targets for the increased hiring and promotion for members of the target groups, namely, women, migrants of non-English-speaking background, Aborigines and (in a 1983 amendment) people with physical disabilities.[5]

The legislation in New South Wales was based on the implementation of affirmative action in the United States, but was designed to be particularly Australian in flavour. This is of course an elusive concept, but in general terms this meant that the New South Wales legislation would avoid what were generally seen (unfairly, in my view) to be the excesses and exaggerations of the American experience. Specifically, the legislation avoided any provision for what was termed 'hard' affirmative action in the form of 'quota' hiring, that is, direct preferential hiring. Rather, it was intended that the exercise of preparing a statistical analysis of the workforce in each authority, and then of developing numerical or percentage targets for improving representation, would have the effect over time of improving the profile of the organisation by a process of slow institutional change, both in attitudes and in procedures.[6]

The Director of Equal Opportunity in Public Employment appointed in September 1980 was Alison Ziller, who was born in Great Britain and had migrated to Australia some ten years previously. Ziller had worked in the New South Wales public service in a number of capacities, including positions at the Anti-Discrimination Board and the Public Service Board. She had been a colleague of Dr Peter Wilenski, the director of a review of the New South Wales Public Administration that had given rise to the New South Wales EEO legislation. She had written the report for the review on EEO, entitled *The Affirmative Action Handbook*.[7] She was thus well qualified to take up the position of Director, although her appointment was delayed by the opposition of the head of the Premier's Department, Gerry Gleeson, on the well-founded suspicion that she was likely to be an effective implementer of the legislation.

I joined the office of the Director of Equal Opportunity in Public Employment (DEOPE) in March 1981, as the first permanent Senior Adviser. I was thus part of the early years of the implementation of the EEO programme, when the question was still open as to whether or not this piece of law would have any real impact on practices within the New South Wales public service. The crucial variable was the attitude of the then New South Wales Premier, Neville Wran. Wran had been elected in 1976 on a platform that included a promise of introducing EEO legislation. In his first year in office he established the Anti-Discrimination Board, with legislation that provided for redress against complaints of discrimination on the grounds of sex, race and marital status. (Physical and mental disability — 1983 — and sexual preference — 1985 — were added as grounds as the legislation gained credibility and strength.) Wran was a powerful and charismatic figure, who led Labor to victory in New South Wales the year after the traumatic defeat of Labor nationally in 1975. The coalition of constituencies that Wran put together — including unions, progressive inner-city yuppies, business-people, women, Aborigines and members of the several migrant communities — was to become a model for Labor leaders in the decade that followed, culminating in victories for Labor in the states of Victoria, South Australia, Western Australia, and, in 1983, the federal government led by Bob Hawke.

Wran was seen as an authentic working-class hero. This was a bit disingenuous on his part as although he was from a poor family, he had actually received a law degree from Sydney University and had become a successful and wealthy barrister before entering politics. He prided himself on his ability to fraternise with all strata of the population, and to rub shoulders with wharfies in pubs as well as with bankers and financiers. His style of leadership within the party was based upon his personal prestige, and his notoriously fearsome temper when crossed. The government owed its victory to Wran's personal qualities, and so he was able to exert power over his cabinet colleagues by virtue of saying what he wanted in a very loud voice, as required.

In addition to his personal qualities, Wran's power within the Labor Party stemmed from his successful balancing act between the Right and the Left. This he maintained in part in a complicated partnership with Gerry Gleeson, head of the Premier's Department, whom he used as a kind of Alsatian to attack policies and persons who were perceived as being too far to the left. The struggle between Right and Left often took the form of Wran permitting Gleeson certain victories, but then overriding him on other issues. On the appointment of Alison Ziller, Wran overrode Gleeson, giving a first indication that he intended to take the EEO legislation seriously.

The first element in the implementation of Part IXA was the requirement that the departments and authorities of the New South Wales state administration submit their EEO management plans by a stated date — 1 September 1981 for departments and 1 June 1982 for declared authorities.[8] In order to do so, organisations had to hire an EEO officer, known as a Coordinator. The role of DEOPE under the legislation was to advise and assist organisations. We did this by helping them to hire appropriate personnel to prepare the plans, by providing seminars on data collection to assist Coordinators in carrying out the statistical survey to establish a baseline profile of their workforce, and by giving moral, political and emotional support to the Coordinators.

Being the first of their breed in the New South Wales public service, the EEO Coordinators were invariably viewed with enormous suspicion by everyone, including those who had initially hired them. I was deeply familiar with this particular bureaucratic mechanism, from my own pro-fessional experience in running an innovative programme in quite a different context. (From 1970 to 1980 I directed the Experimental Stud-ies Program at Barnard College, Columbia University, in New York, an experiential learning course which grew out of the experimental educa-tion movement of the late 1960s.) The way it works is this: an organis-ation is required — by some external or internal (political) force — to accept a programme that it basically perceives as unnecessary, stupid, wasteful of resources and/or subversive. It hires the person who will preside over the programme, and then proceeds to marginalise and disempower that person by displacing the responsibility and the blame for the idea of the programme onto the poor innocent who has agreed to be in charge of it. The new Coordinators, thus manipulated, were in a state of bewilderment.

The Coordinators required enormous reserves of support and encour-agement, especially because the departments and declared authorities were not at all inclined to take the EEO legislation seriously. Under the 1979 Public Service Act, the departments had been given a great deal of freedom to manage themselves, especially in the area of recruitment and promotion of staff above the entry ('base grade') levels. The authorities had always enjoyed such freedom by virtue of operating under their own legislation.[9] All organisations viewed the passage of the EEO legislation as a form of window dressing and therefore the initial letters to heads of organisations, and the dutiful visits of the DEOPE to each of them, were greeted with derision. The first months of the operation of our office were therefore a kind of phony war, with all players in effect waiting to see what position the Premier would take.

When it became clear that organisations were dragging their heels and showing no intention of meeting their deadlines, the DEOPE decided to appeal to the Premier for his support. I was asked to draft two alterna-tive memoranda, one indicating mild concern at the delays in lodgement of the initial EEO management plans, and the other forceful, using phrases like 'I view with grave dismay . . .' After her meeting with the

Premier, the Director returned in triumph, reporting that Wran had pushed aside the weaker memo and had signed the tough one.

The effect of the memo was magical. I remember remarking on the power of the written word, seeing the effects of the one piece of paper on the attitudes and the behaviour of the heads of the organisations. The EEO plans began to be written, and they began to appear in our office. It was evident that the Premier had come down on the side of the Director and of the legislation, and that people understood that he meant business. This experience of the first test of Wran's commitment to the legislation was repeated many times over the period from 1981 to 1986, when Wran retired from the Premiership. This was my first lesson in the power of legislation and how it was linked, in the New South Wales context, to political power. The office of the DEOPE had the backing of the Premier, and so power flowed to us in an invisible but palpable stream.

However the power, such as it was, was not exerted equally. The organisations making up the New South Wales public administration were enormously individual and distinct and so, too, were their attitudes toward the EEO legislation. In the first phase of implementation, the organisations scheduled under the amendment were the departments and the authorities, some 103 in number. (In 1983 universities and colleges of advanced education were added as well, but that is another story.) These included enormous operational bodies such as the Department of Main Roads, the Water Board and the State Rail Authority, ranging in size from 5000 to over 50,000 employees throughout the state. Their employment practices had gone virtually without outside scrutiny for many years and were based principally on seniority, controlled by powerful trade unions, and, in many instances, on nepotism and local networks. In the Department of Main Roads, for example, recruitment was carried out locally across the state in some 70 different offices, operating without any central guidelines or controls and with recordkeeping in the form of individual personnel cards. One of the jokes that circulated in the early years of the legislation, repeated only half-facetiously, was that equal employment opportunity would come to the Water Board when they started to hire the daughters, as well as the sons, of the current workforce.

The Department of Education was an especially tough nut to crack. This was, and is, one of the most powerful of the state agencies, controlling at that time approximately 25 per cent of the state's budget each year, and employing some 46,000 teachers and 12,000 administrative staff members to run 2300 schools across the state. The Department was organised into ten regional areas of administration. But real power remained at the centre, controlled by Head Office. The state depended upon the Department's orderly administration of the annual Higher School Certificate (HSC) examination, which was the gateway to further study for all students in the state in both private and public schools. As I learned when I joined the Department, any proposed measure which could be portrayed as threatening to the orderly conduct of the schools, and especially of the HSC exam, could be derailed without much difficulty.[10]

The progress of the EEO legislation, then, was uneven. In the departments, where some reform to personnel practices had already taken place, introducing EEO principles was easier and the atmosphere more receptive. For example, as noted earlier, promotion on the basis of merit rather than seniority had been established by the 1979 Public Service Act. In the declared authorities, where seniority remained sacred and personnel practices a matter of long tradition, the introduction of EEO principles was initially strenuously resisted. But it was my observation that the reception of EEO was also, in part, a function of a number of other variables: the kind of services the department or authority provided; the professional makeup of the staff, and therefore, the organisational ethos; and perhaps most crucially, the politics and commitments of the senior executive officer of the organisation.

Each department or authority had quite a distinct history and organisational climate. For example, the Corporate Affairs Commission, a department, was peopled by attorneys and other officers committed to sleuthing out frauds in the corporate sector. They prided themselves upon being tough and were highly resistant (as was perhaps predictable) to being themselves subject to any kind of investigation or inquiry. The Attorney-General's Department on the other hand was, over time, more receptive. While also peopled by attorneys, especially at senior levels, officers of the department were more sympathetic to the idea of using the law for purposes of social change. In addition, they were always ready for a good debate and could see the point of a coherent argument.

One of the standard points in the DEOPE rhetoric was that in order to develop policies that delivered services to the public that were both effective and appropriate to the needs of a diverse citizenry, it was important to ensure that members of the public administration included people from a range of backgrounds — migrant; Aboriginal; women, of all ethnicities; and people with physical disabilities — who could contribute to the design of such policies.[11] I remember addressing groups of senior management at the Attorney-General's Department and seeing a response on their faces (later confirmed in private conversations) that indicated that they saw the force of this argument, and even agreed that this was in effect their responsibility as public servants and as drafters of social policy legislation. No such receptive response lit up the faces of the dreaded legions at the Corporate Affairs Commission, at least in the early years. They remained stony-faced and, in practice, resisted implementing the legislation as long as they could get away with it.

The progress of implementing EEO in New South Wales can be

traced through the annual reports of the DEOPE which were lodged each year in Parliament as a chapter of the Annual Report of the Anti-Discrimination Board.[12] The first stage for each organisation was filing the EEO plan with our office. The initial plans were superficial and easy to pick apart. The statistical analysis of the workplace was in some cases incomplete. In others it was adequate as to the data but astounding in the interpretation. The next step in the establishment of the power of the DEOPE was how the the initial plans were treated. We read each one and graded it as though it were a term paper, sending back a letter to the head of the organisation which read, in effect, B– for effort and D for content: do it again, please.

We later learned that these letters from the DEOPE, which we spent hours gleefully composing, and which were written in a style that was very far from the cramped and convoluted prose of ordinary public service correspondence, were passed from hand to hand by heads of organisations at their monthly meetings. It became over time a matter of prestige to have received a letter from the Director that praised an organisation for some EEO initiative or other, and a matter of embarrassment if the head of the organisation had once again been rapped over the knuckles. Most of the plans were sent back to be redone. Eventually the fact that one's EEO plan had been found satisfactory by the Director, was incorporated into the public sector as a sign of good management. This effect must, in part, have depended upon the close-knit community of the New South Wales public service, where reputations and the opinion of peers counted in the balance.

But some organisations resisted the pressure. Foremost among these was the Department of Education. That the EEO management plan for the Department of Education remained unsatisfactory for longer than that of almost any other organisation appeared to leave its senior management unmoved. The Director-General of Education, R. B. (Bob) Winder, composed letters back to the Director that were fully equal to hers in bureaucratic power, although couched in more traditional language. In them, in effect, he repeatedly challenged the power of the DEOPE to force the Department into compliance.

The heart of the EEO issue for the Department of Education was and had been for many years the imbalance in the distribution of women teachers. (In this narrative I am leaving aside what was in many ways a more crucial but more difficult struggle for the recruitment and promotion of Aboriginal teachers.) Women teachers, who comprised 57 per cent of the service, had over the years been underrepresented in the promotions positions that carried power and prestige in the schools: executive teacher or department head, deputy principal and principal. These senior positions led, via the position of inspector, to power in regional and central administration. The male domination of the teaching service at senior levels (as with school systems elsewhere) had been documented in reports of the Anti-Discrimination Board and widely criticised. The EEO legislation was the perfect vehicle to overcome this, at least in theory. But in practice this required agreement among the DEOPE, the Department of Education and the powerful Teachers Federation trade union to the dismantling of the system of appointment by seniority that had shaped the Department for many years.

Such an agreement seemed difficult, if not impossible. The primary obstacle was a standoff between the DEOPE and the Director-General of Education, which took the following form. The Department had proposed an initial break with seniority in its revised EEO management plan. (An initial plan with no significant changes to personnel procedures had been rejected summarily early in the process.) Ten per cent of the promotions positions were to be allocated for selection by merit rather than by seniority. Forty per cent of the positions were to be allocated to qualified women teachers in a system of direct preference, as an affirmative action measure. The remainder of the system would remain intact, with positions allocated on seniority as in the past.

This was the plan that the DEOPE vetoed in the first instance, for a series of complex reasons. One of these was the Director's concern about the extent of the power of the provisions of Part IXA. The legislation in New South Wales authorised the setting of numerical goals and targets but not of 'quotas'. The 40 per cent provision appeared to be a stronger form of affirmative action than had previously been authorised under the amendment for other EEO plans. And it was clear that there were activist male teachers in the teaching service who were prepared to take court action immediately after the introduction of any affirmative action measure. It appeared safer for DEOPE to ask the Department to amend its own act, rather than to test the strength of our own legislation. (There was a precedent for this. In the case of Aboriginal teachers, the Education Commission Act had been amended to provide for absolute preference for an indefinite period. From the point of view of the Department, however, it would be much more difficult to convince the cabinet of the need for affirmative action on behalf of women than for Aborigines, where the need was so glaring — in 1988, for example, only 53 out of more than 46,000 teachers were Aboriginal.)

Another concern was the vagueness of the provision in the Department's plan for a 10 per cent merit 'slice' of promotions, as it was termed colloquially. What positions would be covered by this provision and how would they be selected? The DEOPE took the view that the introduction of a system of merit should have a self-evident logic to it. For example, it would make sense to introduce merit selection at the level of principals, as the chief leaders in the schools.

The scope for resolving these policy differences was diminished by the souring of relations between the Director and the Director-General of Education. Each felt aggrieved. The Director-General felt that his department had taken enormous steps toward meeting the requirements of the legislation, yet the DEOPE did not appear to give this effort much credit and refused to approve the plan. The Director, meanwhile, envisaged a sweeping reform to the promotions system that would remove seniority altogether. She saw the 40 per cent direct preference provision as a stop-gap measure that preserved some of the worst features of seniority. This was in a context in which the DEOPE had succeeded in convincing other, equally tradition-bound branches of the public service, such as the Police Force, to abandon seniority progressively in favour of merit promotions. The situation was not improved when the Education Minister and the Director-General decided to launch the unapproved EEO management plan at a very public occasion as an official plan of the Department. The Director was invited, and she attended, but the atmosphere at the launch was frosty.

In the middle of this standoff, I was recruited by the Department of Education to take up the newly created position of Leader of their EEO Unit. This was a middle management position, supervising the two existing EEO Coordinators, one responsible for the Education Teaching Service and the principal author of the EEO management plan, Kerry Hyland, and the other, Susan Harben, responsible for the Public Service staff of the Department. As Leader of the Unit I had in effect been poached by the Department with a view to acting as a bridge or mediator between my former and current employers. (Ironically the Department had agreed to create the position of Leader under strong pressure from the DEOPE as a means of forcing the organisation to upgrade the status of EEO. This was in line with a standard policy of DEOPE on the well founded theory that the more senior the EEO positions in an organisation, the more power and authority the programme could wield.)

As it turned out, the Department's ploy worked. After much negotiation we came up with a revised set of strategies for the EEO management plan, a three-part reform which became known as the package. The Director-General, my boss, the Director of Industrial Relations (Geoffrey Baldwin), the EEO Coordinator (ETS), and myself began a year-long campaign to 'sell' this revised version of the EEO strategies to the Minister, the DEOPE, the Teaching Service and the Teachers Federation.

Part one of the package was the promotion of principals by 'comparative assessment'. The system of placing principals in schools according to their number on the seniority list was to be replaced by a system of recommendations and interviews which would give rise to a merit list where candidates were rated according to a series of criteria. The system of interviews was elaborate, organised in each of the ten regions, with the rating list then 'moderated' by a kind of supercommittee at the centre. The net effect would be to open the positions of principal to candidates who might have been assessed as eligible for promotion in the last one or two years, whereas under the old system those taking positions had been waiting patiently on the list for up to fifteen years or more.

Part two was the affirmative action measure for women teachers encompassing 40 per cent of the promotions positions below the level of principal. The method of selecting these women was discussed and refined to avoid any taint of favouritism. Male teachers, who for years had found ways to manipulate the seniority system in order to place themselves in line for what were seen as the plum positions in the service, were deeply suspicious of how the 40 per cent preference was going to operate. The method devised was as follows: the women teachers on the relevant promotions list for each category of appointment were constituted as (in effect) a subset of the seniority list, and for each ten positions, four (that is, names lying at positions 1, 4, 7 and 10 in the group of 10) were to be 'first offered' to the most senior women.

Part three was a provision to remove the service undertaking which had been a requirement for permanency under the system. The EEO statistics had shown that many women had refused to sign the undertaking, which pledged their readiness to serve anywhere in the state, due to domestic responsibilities. To forfeit permanency meant also to forfeit the right to promotion, to superannuation (pension rights) and of course to job security. The rationale for jettisoning this provision was that in practice the Department went to enormous trouble to accommodate the geographical requirements of teachers, and in any case the Education Commission Act provided the Director-General with the powers to move teachers with or without their having signed a pledge. This measure would permit a significant number of temporary teachers, 80 per cent of them women, to become permanent.

This was the package that eventually won Cabinet approval and was signed into law in May 1987. (For the sake of clarity, I have omitted some details of what was an extremely complex reform.) The story of the coalition that was forged to sell the package is the story of an extraordinary alliance of femocrats and bureaucrats, each bringing to the campaign a particular, and not necessarily shared, set of objectives. The DEOPE wanted to reform the promotions system of the Education Department along the lines of other EEO reforms in the state, and to have its authority recognised by the Department without jeopardising the power or the reputation of the state's EEO programme. The Director-General wanted to accommodate the requirements of the EEO legislation without threatening the centralised control over the running of the schools that he saw as key to maintaining the standard of public education. And of course he wanted to protect the power of the centre as against the regions, the schools and the local communities. The Director of Industrial Relations, Geoff Baldwin, wanted a progressive reform that would not disrupt the smooth industrial relations he had achieved with the Teachers Federation.[13] And the EEO officers wanted to ensure that the reform to the promotions system actually benefitted women teachers in a concrete and measurable way.

The motives of the then Minister of Education for New South Wales, Rodney Cavalier, are harder to summarise. He was a complex character: of Italian origin, he was nonetheless hostile to the multicultural mode of celebrating ethnicity that was official Labor Party policy. He was passionately committed to the defence of public education and spent much of his time as Minister travelling around the state visiting schools and showing the flag, as he put it. Cavalier saw himself as a classicist and student of history, was fanatical about watching and playing cricket (the latter pretty badly, I am led to believe), and was notorious for his public animosity to feminism and feminists. In a battle waged within the Labor Party in the 1970s for affirmative action to increase the number of women standing for Parliament and holding positions of influence within the Party, Cavalier had resolutely opposed the measures and coined the term 'gender fascists' to refer to their proponents. He was therefore an unlikely candidate to sympathise with, let alone preside over, the introduction of affirmative action for women teachers.

But on Cavalier's personal staff, and on the permanent staff of the Minister of Education, were several feminists who had been part of the longstanding campaign in New South Wales for women's educational opportunities. While Cavalier took great pleasure in mocking his feminist advisers and their convictions, he was nonetheless capable of grasping the importance of some of their advice on the need for female role models in the schools, the need for excellence in the leadership of the school system, and the need overall for flexibility in school staffing. He was prepared, too, to pay attention to the impassioned arguments of the Director who spent many long hours lobbying him on the need for change in the Department of Education.

Among Cavalier's more admirable qualities were a capacity to listen and to absorb an argument, and the ability to change his mind and his policies once convinced — often for less than admirable reasons, of course, including the electoral main chance — that the new policy was worth pursuing. In addition, he was a very tough player in the party and the Parliament, committed, like most of his colleagues, to winning. Once he made up his mind, he was unshakeable. This firmness turned out to be an enormous asset.

Cavalier presented the package of reforms to the Cabinet, which referred it, in turn, to a sub-committee, where, some assumed, the measure would die. But in fact the sub-committee was convened by the Minister of Health, Peter Anderson, who had progressive views. He duly invited the Minister to present his proposal. And the Minister, in turn, invited the team that had been selling the package, namely, the Director of Industrial Relations, myself, and my colleague, the EEO Coordinator, to address the committee and to answer their questions. The Ministers present appeared to be sympathetic to the need for reform of the system. One with direct personal experience mentioned the problem of 'dead wood', namely, people appointed as principals so far toward the end of their careers that they were in effect retiring on the job, much to the detriment of the students. And no one present appeared to be opposed to the idea of taking some direct measure to ensure a greater representation of women in promotions positions.

We presented the statistics on the current distribution of women in the system, and on the projected future distribution given the placement of women on the promotions lists (well to the bottom, due to loss of seniority for time out in childbearing and childrearing) and the projected retirement ages of the women.[14] And we explained the 40 per cent as a minimum figure that would begin to redress the imbalance. One of the Ministers then posed the question that had come up over and over again in discussions of the package. Would it not be fairer simply to establish two lists, one of men and one of women, and take each name off the top of the lists in alternation? Whenever this question was asked, I would simply pause and wait until the questioner exclaimed, as this one did, 'Hang on, that's 50 per cent!' Nothing more needed to be said. The laughter in the room expressed relief that we were not asking for a half or, indeed, a majority share of the positions.

An incident during the cabinet sub-committee hearing that stays with me occurred in the middle of the meeting, when the tea was brought in by a 'tea-lady'. Looking embarrassed, the Chair of the committee remarked that they had equal opportunity in his department, and that there were also tea-men on duty. There was a moment of tense silence, until I replied, with a smile, 'There's no need to be defensive, Minister.' This produced a roar of laughter all around. The Director-General later told me that this incident was probably a turning point. At that level, he said, they were basing their decisions as much on who was bringing the proposals forward as on the content. My willingness to laugh reassured them that my team and I were not extremists, seeking the defeat of the Labor Government, and they were willing to trust us.

The sub-committee approved the package and then returned the matter to the Cabinet. Weeks went by, with agonising phone calls to the Premier's Department to ask if the measure had been put on the agenda yet. The fear was that the head of department, Gerry Gleeson, who controlled the agenda, would simply arrange for the measure to die via delay. Finally the word came that the matter was on the agenda, and then that it had passed. There was a last-minute attempt by the Labor Council, prompted by the Teachers Federation, to dissuade the Premier from approving the measure. (The Federation objected to the allocation of principals' position on merit, not to the 40 per cent for women teachers. In private Federation president Jennie George saw the change as inevitable and did not really object to it; but she was sworn to uphold the union's position on defending seniority.) But this failed and the amendments to the legislation were officially gazetted in May, to take effect as of the staffing operation which began on 1 July 1987.

When the package came into effect, reactions seemed at first to be subdued. But soon a very vocal group of right-wing male teachers began a campaign against the 40 per cent measure. They gathered staff signatures in schools, pressured women teachers against accepting the positions when they were offered and influenced some colleagues to isolate and to harass women teachers who would benefit personally from the legislation. A public debate began in the press. There seemed to be a general degree of acceptance for the principles of the package. There was, however, a clear indication that the Liberal and National Parties making up the opposition coalition considered the 40 per cent to be an excess caused by Labor Party ideology. They signalled very loudly that should they come to power, the 40 per cent would have to go.

Meanwhile the projected figures of the number of women teachers who would actually benefit from the measure turned out to be low. The EEO research had indicated that the 40 per cent would probably be a high estimate. Some women teachers would not accept the positions offered to them, either for reasons of geography or of reluctance to take a position not actually offered to them on 'merit'. (Of course under the previous seniority system no one had 'earned' a promotion in that sense. All teachers had demonstrated comparable merit on being accepted into the teaching service. Thereafter promotions had been acquired via longevity in the system and it was chiefly women who had to sacrifice longevity to the demands of childrearing.) But of the deputy principals' positions offered to women under the 40 per cent measure in the first year — just over 50 positions — all but one were taken up. So much for research! It was clear that the year-long debate about affirmative action and the long years before that of campaigns on behalf of women teachers had had their effect. There was a generation of teachers who were happy to accept the measure of redress that had been won on their behalf.

The victory, however, was short-lived. On 19 March 1988 the Labor Government lost power to the Liberal–National coalition. Within a week of winning the election, the new government announced that the 40 per cent affirmative action measure would be withdrawn. They also announced the sacking of the newly appointed Director-General of Education, who had been selected by the outgoing minister, Rodney Cavalier. Privately, the new Liberal Minister for Education assured the Department of his support for EEO measures in general, but said that the government had been obliged to get rid of the 40 per cent goal as this had been a very public campaign promise. The government looked to instituting merit promotions system-wide over the coming decade, and would rely on the EEO unit for suggestions as to how this should be implemented. Shortly thereafter, the capacity of the EEO unit to provide useful advice was severely reduced, with a cut in staff numbers from twenty-three positions to three. These events facilitated my decision to leave the Department of Education in April 1988, permanently, as it turned out. As of this writing, seniority has been abolished and the Department is being restructured. It remains to be seen what the outcome of the changes will be for the prospects of women.

The account I have given here is a bare-bones narrative, which leaves out many aspects of the story (including, as noted, the role of the union and of the Anti-Discrimination Board of New South Wales). In part this is due to the limitations on my own experience and for the sake of simplifying the narrative. But some material is omitted because certain aspects are painful to recall and politically unwise to make public. I will refer to elements of these difficult areas in the comments which follow.

The first general point to make is about the pull of institutional loyalties and institutional socialisation on women, and the impact of these upon an ideal form of behaviour inspired by feminist solidarity. One of the effects of becoming a femocrat is that one is inevitably drawn into the politics and the ethos of the organisation for which one is working. This seems a truism, yet it is crucial to understand.

The EEO officers working for the Department of Education had two choices. If they gave their allegiance wholeheartedly to the organisation, then inevitably their behaviour and their decision-making favoured the interests of the organisation. This was at the expense of an ability really to offer inside information to femocrats located elsewhere, for example, inside the DEOPE or the Minister's office. If they gave their allegiance to the DEOPE on the ground that this is where the power to improve the situation of women workers lay, then they were viewed with intense suspicion, and treated as members of a fifth column to whom delicate and sometimes sensitive matters of high policy could not be divulged. In effect, they were rendered powerless.

The navigation of these shoals was a constant matter of judgment, and thus no interaction with one's sisters outside of the organisation (or, for that matter, inside of it) was free of calculation. All transactions were subject to the same editing, caveats about confidentiality, and about deniability: 'You never heard this from me.' As with other bureaucratic transactions, communication among femocrats was carefully managed and controlled, and the degree of trust among us was thus always at best partial. The strain of this conflict of loyalties took its toll, especially on femocrats whose entry to the bureaucracy had been primarily motivated by a commitment to feminist ideals.

The second point is the difference it made as to what forms of feminism one was espousing. There was a continuing debate in New

South Wales during the decade of EEO activism as to whether or not this was 'really' feminism. EEO and affirmative action were seen as imports from the United States, and were highly suspect on this ground alone. In addition, the structure of the EEO legislation placed it squarely within a tradition of liberal democratic reform. To the extent that the overall impact of EEO implementation in the public sector was on procedures — improvements, for example, in the criteria for selection and in methods for recruitment and appointment of personnel at all levels — it was seen as reformist, limited in scope and having little or nothing to do with the specific interests and needs of women as a group. Of course, the 40 per cent affirmative action measure for women in the Department of Education tested this, as it was clearly an out-and-out measure of redress specifically to women teachers. The reluctance of DEOPE initially to espouse this, for reasons outlined earlier, opened that office (unfairly, in my view) to a charge of betraying feminism or, more broadly, of never having been really feminist in the first place.

A third point is about the fortunes of feminist aspirations as linked to the fortunes of political parties and leaders. Clearly the EEO initiative in New South Wales was linked to Neville Wran and to the power of the Labor Party. The fragility of this strategy is indicated by the outcome of the story. The Labor Party federally and in the states has committed itself in policy terms to a range of feminist objectives, from affirmative action to child care — although not to equal pay for work of comparable value — as a frank exercise in increasing its electoral margin through the votes of women. The women's movement, in turn, has taken advantage of this to claim its dues for women's issues where Labor has come to power. This is a risky fate for feminism. Yet what other path forward is there?[15]

A fourth point concerns the kind of power accorded to femocrats and the kind of power wielded by them. In an early discussion with my boss, Geoff Baldwin, at the Department of Education, he remarked to me that in his first year as Director of Industrial Relations he had made perhaps hundreds of phone calls to his colleagues, the Regional Directors of Education, with requests for them to take action of one kind or another. Very often these were for things they were most reluctant to do. Technically my boss was exactly at the same bureaucratic level as the Regional Directors. Yet it was known that he was close to the Director-General and often was phoning at the latter's request. In only one case during the year had he needed to phrase the phone call more strongly than saying things like, 'Look, Ralph, I wonder if you'd mind doing X?'

This style of wielding power was very far indeed from that to which I was accustomed in the office of the DEOPE where, even with the derived power of the Premier behind us, we wrote stern letter upon stern letter before getting action, and often had to invoke the personal wrath of the Minister concerned before our requests were heeded. Was this a function of the gender difference? Or was it the bureaucratic response to the outsider versus the insider? It ran through my mind that each male bureaucrat, whatever his style, had a tradition of thousands of years of bureaucratic power behind him, stretching back to Babylon. The senior women groped for an appropriate style. They eschewed the nurturing role for fear of being treated as a mother (with all of the ambivalences this evokes) rather than a boss. But they were unable really to use the full range of male styles of leadership, especially the angry father mode of exerting authority through unpredictable fits of rage. When used by women against men this evoked a particularly deadly form of rage in return.

What was effective, in my experience, was a form of alliance between femocrats and traditional bureaucrats where our interests ran parallel. In this context it was quite possible to be oneself in manner and even in outrageous language, because one's authority as a feminist expert was recognised and even sought in the context of a particular initiative such as the one I have described here. Here one's gender was, as it were, legitimate. I was speaking as an official advocate for women and therefore arguments from me had weight.

In a curious way, then, the power of femocrats stemmed from their explicit orientation and role, and this provided a good deal of freedom to manoeuvre. Needless to say, however, the power thus wielded was extremely limited in scope. It was hedged about by the priorities of the organisation as a whole and by the degree to which one's own feminist projects could be fitted in within this larger set of priorities. The struggle was always to extend the areas within which one's gender experience and expertise were recognised by the men who continued, over all, to set the agenda.

Bearing in mind my comments at the beginning of this chapter on the specificity of national differences and their impact upon feminist interventions, what can be drawn from this experience that is useful in developing an internationally relevant body of feminist theory?

Do we need to reconsider the slogan 'the personal is the political'? In its original usage, this was a feminist statement about the need to see the operations of power in so-called private situations such as marriage. But in the context of women wielding a modicum of political power in a system still under strong patriarchal control, it may now be necessary to think about the political as the personal, and to ask why, among women, the political gets so personal? In the context of the EEO experiment in New South Wales, there has been a widespread expression of disillusionment with femocrats among feminists. What is our expectation of women, and especially of feminists, with a degree of power?

In thinking about this question, I found myself looking back to the experience of consciousness-raising and to some of the comments by Adrienne Rich about the difficulties of mother–daughter relationships in members of the generation of feminists growing up in the 1940s.[16] At least among white feminists there was an experience of finding within feminism relationships among women that were free of the conflicts and the ambivalence that had characterised relationships among women within the family and in friendships. Feminism seemed to promise a world of nurturance and acceptance, a redress of the hurts suffered by women at each others' hands in an era when female solidarity was culturally impossible.

The entry of women into positions of significant power, even when this is accompanied by a feminist programme and personal commitment, has meant that relations among women of this kind cannot, structurally speaking, partake of the quality of nurturance and mutual acceptance that was part of the feminist utopia. The pull of institutional loyalties seems inevitably to tug against the ties of ideological sisterhood. Is this why conflicts among femocrats or other professional and official feminists such as Women's Studies scholars or feminist politicians have such a painful quality?[17]

Are there lessons from the Australian experience for the women's movement in the United States and elsewhere? As noted, the path followed by feminists in New South Wales and in Australia in general has been reliant upon an alliance with the Labor Party, and on a decision to take up bureaucratic positions within state and federal administrations in order to further the interests of women using the power of the state. This strategy obviously relies upon a willingness to accept the constraints of what is politically expedient, that is, saleable to the electorate and to the Party, in the outcomes that can be achieved for women.

Is this an acceptable model for elsewhere? Is it even a feasible model? Recent developments in Great Britain would seem to indicate that political forces to the left of the spectrum are for the moment radically splintered by the extraordinary power being controlled by Margaret Thatcher. In the United States, the Democratic Party seems an unreliable ally for women. But there are many avenues for feminist interventions at state and local levels. Toward the end of the twentieth century it seems futile to argue that feminists should not where possible be seeking to use the political process to further our ends. Indeed Anna Yeatman has argued that at least in the Australian context the only possible feminist politics in the 1990s is a politics of the state.[18]

What are the implications of the New South Wales experience for our theoretical views on power and gender? At the moment it seems to me that gender theory is located within a kind of feminist tower of Babel. The deconstructionists can barely speak to the empiricists and vice-versa (and this failure of dialogue is of course complicated by the debate over the politics of deconstructionism).[19] To some extent, this is the result of success and of specialisation. Feminists have infiltrated the academy and as moles within the disciplines are shaping, and being shaped by, the discourses reigning in each area. The experience of feminist interventions in what is sometimes called the real world, as filtered through the lenses of the several disciplines, gets fragmented and perhaps distorted. Feminism becomes a series of disparate phenomena: women as political leaders or voters in political science analysis; women as bearers of difference in literary theory; women as the embodiment of an alternative morality in psychology; and feminism as epistemology in philosophy.[20]

Meanwhile a generation of feminists has been, in practice, reshaping the meaning of gender through their lived experience as political actors, in an enormous range of different settings: government bureaucracies; trade unions; universities; political parties; corporations; and religious organisations. I have the persistent impression that theory lags radically behind practice and that the experience of these women — the 'first' firewoman, Vice-Presidential candidate, union president, and so on — provides data for a reconsideration of a lot of what has been said in the first round of theorising about gender difference and its relation to organisational structures, socialisation and work experience. This chapter has been an attempt to contribute some experiential data to that investigation. I imagine that much more of this kind of work is needed in order really to rethink our theoretical frameworks about the relationship of women — and particularly of feminist women — to power.

Part III

6 Harvard and New South Wales: feminists in the interstices

This chapter is an edited transcript of a radio programme that I did with Alice Jardine on the Australian Broadcasting Corporation Radio National Series, *The Minders: People in Conversation About Ideas*, on Saturday, 26 July, 1986. The programme was proposed and produced by Penny O'Donnell. Alice was visiting Australia to attend the Australian National University's Institute for the Humanities Conference, which was devoted that year to feminist scholarship.

As colleagues and friends our two paths have crossed many times, most notably in our collaboration on the text of *The Future of Difference*.[1] This particular conversation took place in Sydney and it took off from the themes of our then recently published books on feminist theory[2] to consider the issue of feminist theory and practice as they presented themselves to us in our respective locations within traditionally patriarchal institutions.

The context of our discussion was the debate about the uses of postmodernism and, more specifically, of the work of French theorists such as Lacan, Derrida and Foucault, for advancing a feminist programme of radical change in culture and politics. There is now an important literature on this subject.[3] The discussion that follows is informal, but it places some of the more abstract ideas in the context of our respective intellectual and political trajectories and is, I hope, of value for that reason. I have borrowed the idea of 'interstices' from Teresa de Lauretis (see 'Gender as a Category of Analysis', page 107).

Alice: The book's title is *Gynesis*: *Gyn* for woman, and *sis* in Greek means process. It's about the ways in which certain French thinkers, both male and female, have problematised the words 'woman', 'female', 'feminine', etc. They use the word 'female' or 'feminine' in their work and yet it doesn't seem to have anything to do with women. This has rendered thinking about the relationship between these people's work and feminism very difficult. I think *Gynesis* is important as an intervention in a very particular context, an international context, but primarily Anglo-American and French. The book is intervening in a discussion at a very particular time. It is a time of great dispute, both generally within the philosophical community as well as more particularly within the feminist movement, over a certain number of issues raised by a conflict between what we can roughly call the Anglo-American empirical tradition and continental theory, especially French theory of the last twenty-five to thirty years.

Hester: When you say the Anglo-American tradition, you're talking about a tradition that relies on being able to attach numbers to things. Is that a fair enough way to characterise it? In other words, for something to have validity, it must be empirically verifiable, it has to be predictable in the scientific sense. You have to be able to feel it and touch it, or at least to measure it.

Alice: Right. You tend to work with notions which have not been problematised, like 'experience' and 'truth', 'reality' and 'history'. But all of these categories of knowledge have been largely thrown into question by a certain group of French thinkers over the last few years.

Hester: Can you say a little bit more about these developments in the case of the French theorists that you're taking on?

Alice: Well, for example, in most Anglo-American feminist work we think about the human subject or the human personality as a unified entity with a continuous history, shaped by memory and experience. This concept has been profoundly challenged in France through two disciplines primarily, psychoanalysis and the discipline of semiotics, which is the study of meaning and how meaning is produced. Both disciplines combined have problematised the notion of the human subject by positing simply that the human subject has an unconscious and that this unconscious undoes everything that the empiricist tradition has at different moments claimed as true and universal, across the board for men and women, since the beginning of time. This new kind of subject with an unconscious poses a problem for us, namely, that it is very difficult to figure out how this new kind of subject can be feminist.

Hester: Yes. One of my problems with this body of theory is exactly that issue. It is my suspicion that the death of the unified subject came about just at the historical moment when feminists were deciding that the human subject could be female. I take a conspiratorial view of this new tradition. But tell us more about the analysis in your book. When I read it I thought you were being extremely courageous in taking on all the heavy male dudes like Derrida, Lacan and Foucault. You were essentially saying that the emperor has no clothes in this sense: on the one hand these writers had elevated the status of femaleness by placing a certain notion of the female at the very centre of their theoretical frameworks. But on the other hand there were all these real live females, particularly in Paris, walking around saying, 'No, no, that's not how we experience our femininity, our place in the world and our moment in history.' It was as though the male theorists were saying, in effect, 'You real women, shut up! *We're* going to write about this; we are the authorities on what femaleness and femininity really signify.'

Alice: The gesture behind *Gynesis* was really double. And that's one of the reasons why it gets lots of different kinds of readings. I have been trying to show that Derrida *et al.* suddenly began talking about 'the woman' and 'the feminine' as somehow intrinsic to thinking about modernity, to thinking about the twentieth century; that they did so at the same historical moment the Women's Movement rose up and became increasingly vocal, important and interesting. So the book is a critique of this body of male theory, if you like. But at the same time, it recognises that this particular group of philosophers, semioticians and poeticians has hit upon something which I think really is essential to thinking about the twentieth century. They were the first thinkers to realise that since at least the end of the nineteenth century, all of those qualities which had been devalorised historically as female were beginning to be widely revalorised across the disciplines.

So that's been the difficulty both in writing the book and in the book's reception. I have been trying to convey this double situation. I'm trying both to criticise something and also to say that I think women interested in feminism should take a careful look at it. We need to understand that the subject has been deconstructed, that perhaps dialectical logic doesn't work any more, and that perhaps all of these female qualities are essential to thinking about the twentieth century. For us to keep saying, 'No, no, it's just a male conspiracy,' may keep us from plugging into some of the most radical kinds of contemporary thinking.

Hester: Yes. Essentially you're saying 'Let's not miss the boat' in the sense that we get so angry at male theoretical characterisations of what is female that we lose sight of what is of value in their analysis. But I think the reaction is understandable. After all, we come out of a feminist tradition which says that we're sick and tired of having men define us and pronounce upon what is appropriately 'feminine', rather than giving women the opportunity to say, 'As women we will define ourselves any damn way we please.' I think that in effect you are making a broader point with which I and many other students of feminism would agree, namely, that we need to recognise, however reluctantly, that feminism in fact grows out of the Western tradition. It is well and truly a daughter of Western theory and Western patriarchal categories of thought. What, then, do we do with this understanding? You're really saying, 'Listen sisters, we can't just turn our backs on this.' In fact, we might find ourselves at a crucial conjuncture between feminist theory and postmodern theories of language and of culture.

Alice: Yes. That kind of radical thinking is actually often about thinking 'double', always putting oneself into question. And in this case, it's a way of thinking both critically and also affirmatively at the same time. For me, if there is anything specific to the twentieth century and to what we can call the postmodern, it is that: the capacity to think, not in double binds, but in double synch all of the time.

Hester: Do you mean, along a couple of channels?

Alice: Yes. Along a couple of channels. A few people have said to me that they found it very interesting to read our two books as echoes of one another. Your book concentrates on the Anglo-American feminist tradition and the various phases and developments within that tradition. Mine comes in from left field, in a way, bringing in the French theoretical material and yet simultaneously affirming the tradition that you write about. I keep it as a safeguard, as something I want to protect and valorise, while also critiquing it in a very strong fashion.

Hester: I guess one of the obvious issues is the relationship between feminist theory and feminist practice. I am still completely convinced that the ideas that I outlined in that book, the radical feminist ideas, continue to be at the core of the second wave. That's the heart of it. So you can't get away with not exploring that. We are still spinning out the meaning of that focus within US feminist theory on sexual politics. But at the same time I have felt a kind of impatience with a certain pessimism that seemed to be emerging in the early 1980s which seemed to be keeping sexual politics from becoming a real political programme. Feminist theory seemed to be becoming an internalised navel-gazing exercise instead of proceeding to action: having analysed the culture in this way, how will we in fact intervene to create change?

Perhaps we can turn now to a discussion of our own biographies. How have theory and practice come together for you in your life?

Alice: In the late 1960s and early 1970s I was confused about how to put together all of the things that I cared about. Those things included literature and philosophy, but they also included the civil rights movement and the feminist movement. I felt split apart. I couldn't figure out how to think. Then, in my second year in graduate school at Columbia University, Julia Kristeva, the French psychoanalyst and semiotician, came to Columbia for a year — in 1976 — and I became her research assistant. For me that year was absolutely essential for accumulating the tools I felt that I had been lacking in order to think about putting all of my concerns together. It was also important in terms of my growing commitment to teaching. Right after that I went off to Paris and spent a number of years studying many of the writers who were to appear in *Gynesis*.

When I came back from Paris in 1982 I began looking for a job and I was hired at Harvard University in the Romance Languages and Literatures Department. I was hired in part as a kind of representative of French theory, but also as a feminist theorist. The last three-and-a-half years have been about trying to bring everything together — all of my teaching, the book, my new project — in some kind of workable fashion. I often say to my friends that in order to do that I have to work at two speeds. Working within the institution, I have to work at ... it's not exactly a slower speed, but it's perhaps a more careful speed. This includes helping to set up a Women's Studies programme at Harvard, encouraging the establishment of Women's Studies courses across the disciplines and teaching in the classroom to students who have often never even heard of Women's Studies, let alone ever thought for one minute about feminism and what it might mean for them. Our students often have terribly archaic notions left over from the 1960s about what feminists are doing in various disciplines. This kind of work, of really mainstreaming in a sense within the university, is one part of what I do.

And then there's the other part, which takes place at a higher speed, although again I'm not sure that that is the exact metaphor to use. The higher speed work involves doing things like starting a journal at Harvard called *Copyright*. The first issue will be about this *fin-de-siècle*, the end of the twentieth century, and the various intellectual, cultural and political problems that arise in relation to this event: our relationships to the state, to religion, to all kinds of things.[4] This is what keeps me going intellectually.

Hester: Yes. My story is ... I don't know if it's a similar story! I started out, as you know, as an academic, a historian, and then got immersed in the feminist writings of the second wave as they started coming out in the early 1970s. It seemed to me that the publication of this material was the most interesting thing that had happened, intellectually, in a very long time, and that we ought to start writing about it. But what's happened to me is a certain kind of transformation, because of my life experience of being translated from being a Women's Studies activist, an activist in the academy if you like, which I think is what you're still doing, to being another kind of activist. I'm now in the New South Wales State public service, and my official duties are to implement equal employment opportunity policies in the public sector of the state, that is, within the New South Wales state government administration. And yet I am the same person I was before, namely, a feminist who is trying to explain feminism to people who have very little understanding of it.

Alice: How do you go about doing that?

Hester: It is complicated; one has to operate at a number of levels. Being a proper femocrat means writing policy and chasing files, of course. But a major portion of my job involves talking to an amazing range of people about feminist principles. In this kind of position you have an enormous responsibility to educate people and you have to do it in a patient way. I must say that I don't see it as that different from teaching undergraduates, to tell you the truth, in the sense that you always have to start from where people are. I can give you a very specific example. One of the people who works in my unit is an administrative assistant, a migrant woman from Latin America who is always working on improving her knowledge of English. I noticed today that she was looking at the dictionary. Later on she told me that she had looked up the word 'feminism'. I thought to myself, well done! She hears it from my colleagues and me all day long and she wants to know, what exactly do we mean? And at a number of levels people are saying the same thing to me, 'Well, what exactly does it mean?' Before you can answer them, you have to choose carefully from your array of possible approaches. Are you going to do your song and dance on current statistics on women in the paid work force in Australia and the need for child care? Or are you going to start speaking philosophically about human rights? Or are you going to say to somebody, if it's a man, 'Well, does your wife work?' It's a question of finding a way in. And this has to be calibrated to that person's experience, what they bring to the question, and the expression on their face when they ask you.

Alice: What do you see as the relationship between this terribly nitty-gritty, patient work and your writing?

Hester: I have to tell you that I feel embarrassed, given your sophistication about postmodernism, the death of the subject, and the proposal that universalising discourses are no longer possible, in that I feel as though I am the last liberal. There is certainly a tension between the kind of reformist feminism I practise at work and the utopianism that is expressed in my book. But it seems to me there is also an enormous tension between the goals of feminism as expressed both in my daily work and in my writing, and the world view that is set forth in *Gynesis*. It's quite interesting that people are reading the two books together, actually. Because what you're saying is that you are drawing attention to the enormous questioning that's gone on, philosophically, about the possibility of holding views that are tenets of liberalism. For example, that justice matters; that there is such a thing as truth; and that there is such a thing as an individual with a continuous history, who has a past and who makes autonomous decisions. That set of assumptions underlies liberal theory about the social contract, starting with John Locke, and embracing the entire tradition of the liberal western democracies.

Alice: Well, I think that's why I used the metaphor of working at two speeds. When I work within Harvard University and I am attempting to change the institution I am the other last liberal. I mean, I have to proceed as a subject who believes in truth, justice and experience, and in doing the right as opposed to the wrong thing. Whereas in my writing, and in the material that I read and think about, every term of my daily practice is put into question. Because basically the male theorists I have written about have said that all of the 'emancipatory' discourses that have been handed down to us date, after all, from the European eighteenth and nineteenth centuries. The Master Narratives, the Great Discourses of literature, history and religion are finished in postmodern culture, they say: at least we can no longer unproblematically use those discourses to talk about human liberation. In my most pessimistic moments I say to myself, 'Well, if we can't talk about human liberation, what can we possibly talk about?' So that's why I was very interested when you said you were the last liberal, because I think any feminist working within a Western context and who is attempting to change things at whatever speed or at whatever level has to somewhat identify with the liberal tradition.

Hester: Yes. I think it's a question of what you do with liberalism. I know that in the 1960s a lot of people said it was a hollow force. But I'm now coming to think that really what we're talking about is stretching liberalism — pushing it and forcing it to change its shape to include everything that is excluded, most importantly women, and all people of colour. The hypocrisy of liberalism was that it was the governing philosophy of the imperialist powers who in the name of freedom and equality enslaved and murdered and oppressed the non-white peoples of the world. But now the non-white people of the world are using those same principles very effectively to say, but what about us, our self-determination and our subjectivity? So that's what I think is one of the tensions between your writing and mine. That actually is the basis of the sardonic remark I made earlier, which is in effect that European males announce the death of liberty, equality and truth just at the moment when the rest of the world — the previously excluded groups — are saying, hang on, we want some!

Alice: Yes. I think that's a very good point. But I also think that I have been deeply affected by my encounter with a certain famous tradition of scepticism, where if somebody poses you a question, instead of trying to find the answer you challenge every element of the question. In fact, there are a lot of concepts like liberalism that are both useful and problematic at the same time. I was just thinking as you were talking about the whole issue of pluralism which for years and years has had a very good press. Every good liberal tries to say that they are committed to pluralism and that they will allow the broadest possible range of views to find expression in the institution. But of course the critique that has been carried out by Gayatri Spivak and others of pluralism as a notion has shown that it is always eventually used by those in power to neutralise opposition. I am very pluralist in my everyday activities because I think everyone has a place within feminist theory and practice. And yet at the same time I have to constantly put pluralism itself into question.

This is perhaps the moment to ask each other what we think are the most important issues facing feminists today.

Hester: Ironically, I think a crucial issue for feminists today may be the matter of feminist successes and how we cope with them. Even though you are in a classically academic environment while I am in a public service environment which is fairly political (although I'm not saying your environment isn't saturated with politics, but it's the academic kind of politics), we both have encountered a similar problem, namely, the success achieved by women in entering these institutions. A visible minority of women is no longer asking to be let in, to get a foot in the door. That's still an issue obviously, and will continue to be. But for some privileged women, we *are* in; we *have* a significant and secure place within male-dominated structures. I think that one of the things that you and I share a concern about is this: how have we been using the modicum of power that we now have gotten our hands on? Are we any good at it? I think that this is an enormous issue. I don't mean to exaggerate the degree of power we wield, by the way. But I don't want also to minimise it, either.

Alice: It's a real issue.

Hester: Yes. The classic question, of course, is do women wield power differently from men? One of the things that has become a theme with me is the newness of this experience of women in 'nontraditional' areas of work. I think it was Elizabeth Janeway who said that when a woman picks up a pen she has at least three centuries of tradition to look back on. While she may be a relative newcomer to the production of culture, she's not that much of a newcomer. She can think about Jane Austen, she can think about Aphra Behn. But a woman fire-fighter has a somewhat shorter tradition. And a senior woman bureaucrat has a very short tradition indeed.

Alice: Not to mention an Associate Professor at Harvard . . .

Hester: Yes.

Alice: I'm very concerned about the relationships that we as women develop with one another as we begin working together in various kinds of organisations and institutions. I've been very struck by the way that, in the university, women, older women and younger women, often relive Oedipal types of squabbles. The 'daughters' get very upset with the 'mothers' for all their predictable kinds of shortcomings. And the 'mothers' get jealous or start demanding love or criticising the 'daughters' in familiar ways. I think that one of the enormously difficult things that we're going to have to think about over the next few years will be the institutional kinship systems that are developing among women.

Hester: Absolutely. And the kind of variations on family structures that are reproduced in bureaucratic situations. One of my great fears is, will Daddy turn out to be more reliable than Mommy? Are women finding it easier to draw upon the power and the experience of the senior men than they are to establish really reliable links of mentorship and of trust with the senior women? This could be the case for a whole range of complicated reasons, including competition and jealousy, and perhaps the lack of ease of the senior women in the positions they have only just barely recently won for themselves, at a tremendous psychic cost.

Alice: Do you think that these problems are related to issues of class? Can feminism deal with these issues if only one class of women is represented in the institutions?

Hester: I think that it is one of the major issues that has to be confronted. It is women in Third World countries who are ruining their eyesight making components for the personal computers that feminists in the academy and elsewhere are writing their theory on. So this is a new and complicated form of exploitation. I think that the only way to connect these things is to insist that people doing feminist theory keep focusing upon the the same old bread and butter issues which haven't gone away. If you think about what were the central feminist issues in the 1960s, they were not high falutin', complicated, theoretical issues. Child care, jobs, the sexual division of labour . . .

Alice: Control over one's body.

Hester: Reproductive control, the right to abortion, the right to resist forced sterilisation, equal pay for work of equal value, the right to freedom from rape, to freedom from domestic violence. These are all issues which concern women's self-determination, economic, political and cultural. And this range of feminist issues applies to all women who (as I often say in EEO lectures) occur in nearly every known culture.

What is interesting about the current scene is that women of colour, women of non-English speaking background, and particularly in this country Aboriginal women, are making very original contributions to the feminist agenda. Not all of these groups want to use the word feminism, but certainly they are raising important questions about women's culture and women's entitlements. An example is the point made in Canberra at the Australian National University Institute for the Humanities conference on feminism by Diane Bell, the anthropologist, talking about the task of integrating Aboriginal customary law with Australian law. What she does is to spend a lot of time listening to Aboriginal women talk about their interpretation of what their entitlements are as women under their customary law. That places women's rights in a very different framework to an Australian framework, or rather, to an Anglo-Australian framework. (It would be the *original* Australian framework.)

Alice: Yes. Exactly.

Hester: So that's the kind of thing I think is promising. What's happened is that feminism has had such a worldwide impact. People who came back from the United Nations Conference in Nairobi marking the end of the United Nations Decade for Women were vehement on this point: the international women's movement is not stopping.

Alice: It's not going to go backward.

Hester: It's not going away. The African women who attended the Nairobi conference were participating on the basis of saying, these are the issues that constitute our feminism. Here's what we're concerned with. We want you European women to remember that the central questions in our villages are: will women have to continue forever spending five hours a day carrying water? Will the international feminist movement turn its attention to this kind of issue, issues of sheer economic survival for women?

Alice: These are important questions. This is anecdotal perhaps — but I was recently invited to lecture at the University of Dakar in Senegal. While I was there I went to a couple of women's study groups. Now granted these were educated, university-educated women, but as they were discussing very fundamental issues of reproductive freedom, polygamy, etc., on their desks were copies of books by Gilles Deleuze, Julia Kristeva, and Jacques Lacan . . . I was first surprised and then delighted and encouraged. Most of all it made me want to be quiet and sit back and listen to the ways in which these women were making connections between what we habitually call theory and practice in entirely new ways. It seemed to me that they were doing it a great deal less neurotically than I do. Because I often get stuck on how to put together high theory with nitty-gritty practice. And these women weren't having any trouble doing that at all.

7 The case for feminist optimism

At the time I devised the title, the world had not yet experienced the traumatic disaster at the Chernobyl nuclear power plant. In persisting with an argument for feminist optimism I feel a little bit like Anne Frank. Right up until her untimely death she naively continued to believe in the essential goodness of human nature, in the face of the Nazi concentration camps. How is optimism possible in the modern world, after the Holocaust, after Cambodia, after Three Mile Island and Chernobyl? Yet one of the points I want to make here is the political weight that a stance of optimism carries with it. That is, I want to put onto the agenda of our conventional thinking the notion that a decision for optimism is not a decision only about the empirical reality that confronts us. It is not simply an assessment of the current situation, betting on one result rather than another—that is, a kind of prognosis. It is also part of a commitment to ensuring a particular outcome. As a feminist, I struggle to maintain an optimistic vision of the future, in part as a contribution to making certain that we have a future to move into. This may be a point of connection between feminism and socialism, two 'isms' that I have been accused of favouring both separately and in their interconnections.

My title, then, contains a number of themes. The first is a commitment to optimism itself as a feminist political stance, a belief in the future in order to try and ensure that a future is possible. The second is a sense of optimism about feminism itself. That is, that feminism has made significant gains to date and will continue to do so in the coming years and decades. By feminism, I mean broadly speaking the set of beliefs in the entitlement of women to emancipation, and the political

This chapter was originally delivered as one of the Octagon Lectures at the University of Western Australia in Perth on 10 June 1986.[1]

and social movement which seeks to ensure the achievement of that aim. In defining the term here I find myself deliberately choosing a word that has an archaic flavour. I am saying 'emancipation' (rather than 'liberation')—a word also used in the nineteenth century to refer to the abolition of slavery for the Africans kidnapped in their tens of thousands by the Europeans—in order to connect twentieth century feminism to its eighteenth and nineteenth century forerunners. My sense of optimism is linked to a sense of history and to the place of the movement for women's rights within a historical framework. One can only be optimistic about feminism, in other words, by taking a very long view and by measuring the distance that women have come against the distance that they have had to travel.

Finally, I want to suggest some connections between a stance of optimism—as an attitude or view of the world—and the standpoint of women, to borrow a term from the political theorist Nancy Hartsock.[2] I want to be careful how I put this in that I do not want to be misunderstood. I am not suggesting a stance that proposes any form of biological essentialism or determinism about women or women's nature. But I want to draw out some threads about the relationship between the formation of women's consciousness in modern Western culture and a view of the world that encourages a sense of what is possible, particularly in the area of social and political change, rather than a sense of what is impossible.

Let me say in the first instance what I mean by the success of feminism. All around us are indications of changes in the status of women that can be attributed in whole or in part to the pressures that have been brought to bear on governments by the organised strength of the contemporary women's movement. In most Western democracies legislation has been passed that provides for anti-discrimination agencies and equal employment opportunity measures. Legal reforms have modernised the law of rape and sexual assault and that on domestic violence to give women a more equitable chance in the courtroom against the physical aggression perpetrated on them, and to provide refuges to increase their options to leave dangerous and threatening domestic situations. The access of women to education and training has improved and women have begun to enter a wider range of jobs, including areas traditionally reserved for men, both in the trades and in the professions. Community attitudes toward sexuality have become more tolerant, and the level of debate concerning previously taboo subjects like incest, abortion, prostitution and homosexuality has become more sophisticated. The growth of women's contributions to culture in the areas of film, literature, theatre and other media is marked, as is the flowering of Women's Studies publications in a wide range of academic subjects in the humanities and the social sciences, as well as in some parts of the natural sciences. The intellectual impact of feminism has been formidable. Bob Connell considers that

> we are in the middle of the most important change in the social sciences, and western social thought generally, since the impact of socialist class analysis in the mid-nineteenth century ... The redressers of sexual oppression are currently producing a critical and analytic liveliness and practical relevance unmatched in any other field of social sciences.[3]

The impact of feminism has been worldwide. At the conference held in Nairobi in 1985 to mark the end of the United Nations decade for women, it was evident that the ideas and the aspirations of feminism were now the property of women in most parts of the world who were commencing to shape a feminist agenda within the terms and requirements of their own life situations.[4]

In Australia, in particular, women's interests have been enshrined in bureaucratic structures by means of special agencies. Anne Summers, who summarises these changes, attributes them to the 'electoral power of women'. She writes:

> There are now women's advisory units attached to the Premier's Departments in New South Wales, Victoria, South Australia and Western Australia. The Western Australian Women's Interests Division is the most recent, having been established by the Burke government in 1984. The Northern Territory Women's Advisory Unit was transferred from the Chief Minister's Department in 1984 and now operates as a small unit in the Department of Community Welfare. A women's advisor to the ACT Department of Territories was appointed in 1985. Only in Tasmania and Queensland are there no advisers or councils of women from the community. Some States have also established women's advisors in their Education, TAFE and Health Departments (and, in NSW, in Industrial Relations). Federally, in addition to the Office of the Status of Women in the Department of the Prime Minister and Cabinet, special women's advisory units operate within the Department of Employment and Industrial Relations (the Women's Bureau), the Department of Immigration and Ethnic Affairs (the Women's Desk) and the Department of Education.[5]

Summers also points to the institution of a Women's Budget programme, produced for the first time in 1984, and in 1985 constituting a document of 300 pages, which she (with understandable pride) characterises as 'the most comprehensive path-finder to women's access to government programmes, and the effect of policies on women, ever published by a government'. And finally, women have begun to enter electoral politics in unprecedented numbers. In the United States, there are 1103 female state legislators at this writing, compared to 362 in 1972.[7] The *Sydney Morning Herald* ran a picture on 16 May 1986 of the newly installed cabinet of Norway with its Prime Minister, Gro Harlem Bruntland, and her colleagues, seven women and ten men, a total of 18 (although it is worth remarking that, in that government, the men still had the numbers).[8]

It is customary to dismiss these gains, in some feminist circles, as tokenism. The women's movement has failed to obtain equal pay in practice, despite its establishment on the books in Australia in 1972. It is powerless to stop the increasing poverty of female-headed families (the so-called feminisation of poverty in Western countries). And one can criticise the women's movements of the Western democracies for a failure really to address the economic and social situations of the majority of women. Among American feminists, in particular, there are voices raised in criticism of the tactics pursued by activities for women's rights, for

> pursuing a kind of trickle-down feminism: open up opportunities in
> mayoralties and state legislatures and the U.S. Congress, in higher
> education and the professions, and eventually all women will benefit.[9]

The obstacles to the success of feminism are thus still enormous. Among these one can cite, as an indication of the depth of the problems, the difficulties that women encounter in working effectively and well with one another in the political and bureaucratic arena, in part because of their minority status. In some areas, of course, women have achieved sufficient numbers to constitute a kind of gender caucus, and are able to bring together their interests as women across the boundaries of faction and even of party, for example, in the Federal Parliament and in the Australian Council of Trade Unions, although in the latter body these activities still go on at a very informal and private level. But in bureaucratic structures where women are few and far between above the salary level of keyboard operator and stenographer, for every group of nurturing, mentoring senior women there are, it seems, others who remain threatened by the success of female colleagues and will not reach out a helping hand to them, although their numbers appear to be diminishing. One can still observe a kind of murderous competitiveness between categories and kinds of women: the eye-makeup and 'lippy' brigade despise their punk-haired, boilersuited sisters, and vice-versa.[10]

There is, too, the ever-present danger that initiatives aimed at bringing women into the structures of government and trade unions may create new divisions among women. Marilyn Lake has pointed out that where these measures omit any provisions for changing the structures, whether in the length of the working day, the provision of childcare at the workplace, or additional flexibility in working hours they benefit only certain categories of women. 'In Australia,' she writes,

> most feminist initiatives issuing from government and trade unions have
> not aimed to change the structure of work but to instal women in
> employment on the same terms as men. Affirmative action programmes . . .
> aim to assist women to join the workforce in all capacities and at all
> levels, seemingly without noticing that the main women to be advantaged
> by such a policy are those who share men's traditional privilege of

freedom from domestic responsibilities (either because they are rich or
they do not have children). As equal opportunity becomes equal
opportunism, the result of affirmative action policies could well be the
creation of two classes of women.[11]

The dream of sisterhood among all women then is still elusive, and the
capacity (and eagerness) of some men to exploit and manipulate the
splits among women and groups of women constitutes another barrier to
unity.

As discouraging as the elusiveness of sisterhood is the reception of
the success of women's movement initiatives by the general public.
Anyone who works professionally in the area of women's rights will
understand the point I am making here. One result of the widespread
publicity for feminist ideas in recent years has been a kind of half-baked,
gut-level distorted reception of feminist ideas in the popular press and in
the minds of people whose information about the women's movement
has come only from hearsay and from their own limited experience. The
classic instance of this is what I like to call the 'sample of one' phenomenon. One encounters this in the course of a lecture or workshop in
which one is trying to make a point about the statistics on women in the
paid workforce and to generalise about the experiences of so-called
working women, in order to convey some information about how most
women in this category experience their situation and the attitudes that
they express.

Inevitably the point will be contradicted by an interlocutor who
announces that what the speaker is saying is garbage, and that she is
misleading the audience. The empirical basis for this pronouncement is
usually revealed near the beginning: 'Well, my wife says . . .' Q.E.D. This
is taken as a conclusive refutation of the argument. The sample of one is
inadequate, not only because it is not a sufficiently large sample to be
statistically valid in social science terms, but because it represents not
necessarily what one woman thinks but rather what one woman says to
her husband. The limitations on this kind of data base should be self-
evident.

Another example of distortion is the deliberate and cynical twisting
of feminist ideas in the service of other political objectives. A glaring
example of this arose in New South Wales in the education policy
statement of the Liberal Party issued in 1986. In 1985, the New South
Wales Department of Education was taken to the Equal Employment
Opportunity Tribunal for its policy of corporal punishment for boys, on
the ground that this violated the Anti-Discrimination Act of New South
Wales which prohibits unequal treatment in the provision of services
such as education on the basis of sex. In a development not explicitly
linked to the case but no doubt flowing from it, the then Minister of
Education, Rodney Cavalier, announced that corporal punishment for

boys would be abolished officially by the Department commencing 1987 and advised the Department that schools need not await the deadline in order to begin new approaches to the problem of disciplining unruly students.

Nothing daunted, the Shadow Minister for Education (the Liberal Party's official spokesperson) issued a policy on corporal punishment in schools, indicating that should the Liberals come to power in New South Wales, caning would be restored to the schools but on a non-discriminatory basis: under the Liberals girls would also be caned. The titillating overtones of this were not lost on the media: one early morning radio skit depicted a slathering school master and nubile young school girls . . . In short, in this episode the general grasp on the meaning of anti-discrimination legislation appeared to be woefully thin. The interpretation by the Liberals in this context seemed to be that women are equally entitled, along with men, to the benefits of the Spartan tradition of masculine discipline.

Some of the distorted reception for feminist ideas stems, no doubt, from misunderstanding and lack of proper information and can be dispelled by replacing this distorted version with accurate information about what the agenda of the women's movement has been and continues to be. These are issues that most people would consider to be fair and equitable, such as equal pay, women's access to education, child care, an end to domestic violence and to rape and incest. But this is not true universally: in some cases the more people learn about the real aims of the women's movement, the more hostile they become in their attitudes. But this should not be a surprising outcome.

In the crudest of political terms, the success of feminism may not appear to be and may not actually be in everyone's interest, at least within the terms of their own definitions of those interests. Men who have seen their marriages break down because under the influence of feminist ideas their wives have decided to seek a divorce, may consider the women's movement to be a force for evil. So, too, do some church leaders, who see feminism as an influence that questions the authority of religion in the governing of family life. There is no point in trying to disguise these facts and attempting to make feminism respectable and acceptable to everyone, particularly to people who consider that any change away from the traditional forms of family life is a sign of degradation and social decay.

But what is being eroded in these instances—as well as in the action taken to put an end to more crude and shocking situations of the kind that the women's movement has brought to light, such as rape, wife-battering and father-daughter incest—is the illegitimate power that men have wielded over women by virtue of superior strength and (more powerfully, no doubt) by virtue of a sense of entitlement to authority and decisionmaking within the family, and to access to and control of the sexuality of women as wives and even as daughters. All of this is now in contest as women begin to act on a new sense of their full humanity, their liberties and their right to set the limits and the boundaries of their interactions with others, male and female.

The anger that some men and women feel (and express) toward feminism and the women's movement is connected, I believe, to a sense of loss. In individual circumstances the loss may be palpable: a husband has lost the nurturance and warmth of his wife (for the sake of argument I pass over here the reciprocal loss of wives, when deserted by husbands searching either for self-fulfillment or less edifying objectives). But culturally and socially the loss is of the same order, it is the same phenomenon writ large: something one used to be able to count on, but no longer can, that is, a guarantee that the nurturing and caring work of the world would be carried on by a social grouping who were trained and brought up specifically to carry out this function.

In a world organised by means of the division of labour, the work of caring for and nurturing others has been by and large assigned to women in their roles as wives and mothers. The point has been made *ad nauseum* by feminist writers such as Dorothy Dinnerstein, Jean Baker Miller, Nancy Chodorow and others, that the sexual division of labour in the Western world has included the assignment of nurturing and caring to the female role.[12] In theory this freed men of their obligations in this area in order to carry out their role as centurions. Much ink has been spilled in the elaboration of this point, namely, the objective, rational, steely stance required of men. The need for men to learn to withstand brutal conditions of interpersonal physical violence on the playing fields of Eton and Geelong seemed self-evident in order to prepare them for the manly arts of bureaucratic infighting and of course for war itself.

Now in practice in the modern world it is something of a fantasy to believe that nurturant work is a monopoly held by women. The sex segregation of the labour force is, to be sure, built on this fantasy—that women who become nurses, secretaries and cleaners are simply carrying out their role of domestic nurturance (at appropriate levels of pay) in the paid labour force. This fantasy is however being rapidly demystified by the efforts of militant female trade unionists to replace fantasy with the reality that day care, schooling, the provision of health care for the sick and aging and other areas of 'traditional' women's work are carried out on behalf of the entire community and should be remunerated accordingly. Further, there are areas of socially nurturing work that have traditionally been held by men (for example in medicine). However I am speaking here not of the economic and political reality but of the reception of feminist ideas at the level of general cultural norms.

I believe that the sense that there is a loss of women's nurturance is connected to the entry of women into areas of public life on equal terms with men. Women are entering all areas of work, including some of the most hazardous physically such as firefighting and police work. Equality here has meant equal rights to the risk of death and, in some cases, to death in the line of duty. The fate of Indira Gandhi is a case in point. Here was a woman standing in the same relation to state power as her male predecessors and paying the ultimate price for wielding that power, namely, political assassination.

For me an archetypal event of this moment of transition was the destruction in mid-flight of the American space shuttle Challenger carrying two women, one trained as an astronaut and the other as a teacher (a more traditional role for women), launched into space to risk and lose their lives in a manner traditionally reserved for men. Journalistic accounts of the tragedy struggled with the contradictions embedded in this news story. Pete Hamill wrote a romantic piece in the New York *Village Voice* about the entitlement of Judith Resnick and Christa McAulife to test themselves against the limits of what their bodies and minds could endure, as part of a process which expanded the future options for his own daughters. Resnick and McAuliffe, he wrote,

> didn't board the Challenger alone. Other women had fought, argued, reasoned, persuaded, even died to make it possible for Judith Resnick and Christa McAuliffe to make that flight. These others, brave, tough, beautiful in the best sense of the word, had said that no woman should be denied anything by the accident of gender, including the chance to risk death.[13]

This earnest attempt to assimilate the new emotional requirements of feminism—to move beyond chivalry and the impulse to 'protect' women—on the part of a journalist of the left (or what passes for the left in the United States) seeking to be politically correct in his analysis is, I think, touching but not very convincing.

I am tempted to term Hamill's stance in this article 'patriarchal feminism'. It represents the assimilation of feminist aspirations into the set of values held dear by a death-loving male culture. Equal opportunity, girls, to ride into the eye of the storm! A variation on this theme, just by way of labouring the obvious: press reports on the American bombing of Libya indicated that there had been a number of women pilots on the expedition. A colleague of mine at work told me about this, full of pride and in the expectation that I would take this as yet another sign of women's progress. 'Were the women flying the F-111s?,' said I. No, came the answer: the women pilots were flying the planes that carried out the refuelling of the F-111 bombers in mid-air. A day or so later the full import of this intelligence dawned on me: women's work is never done. The women pilots were feeding the planes that did the actual bombing. What a tribute to the American armed forces, ever the pacesetters in the area of equal rights! These women pilots were provided with a no-lose situation: the opportunity to risk death and retain your role as nurturer into the bargain.[14]

But I digress. To return to Pete Hamill's account of the death of Christa McAuliffe and Judith Resnick: Hamill's analysis omits to take account of the real meaning of the loss of the shuttle which can be linked with the Chernobyl disaster as an instance of the dangerous technology now governing our lives, technology which places all of us at risk by virtue of the carelessness and human error that accompany the ever expanding use of machines more powerful than ourselves but without the intelligence and the ethical sense that we possess, if we could but marshall them. But beyond this, which is a point about the control of technology in a post-nuclear age, Hamill's reaction assimilates McAuliffe and Resnick to a model of male heroism. Underlying this and unstated but crying out for an answer is, if all women become heroes, who will pick up and cuddle their babies for them? Or will they stop having babies altogether?

The simpleminded answer to this lies in the idea of androgyny: we will teach men to nurture in the same way that we are teaching women to take risks and to extend themselves. The evidence that this has begun to happen is visible.

> Even though it may be the result of unemployment, one of the most moving sights these days is to see men caring for their children. One notices them chatting to their toddlers in pushers, grasping preschoolers protectively by the hand as they negotiate the traffic, nursing sick infants on their laps in hospital waiting-rooms and cooing at their babies as they bide their time on railway platforms.[15]

But the question I am asking here is not one about who performs what tasks by gender at the micro-level, although the significance of this shift should not be underestimated. It is a broader one about the future: how can the expansion of opportunities for women in a world now governed by male values be used to turn this into a world that is, in effect, governed by female values?

Let me review the argument I have been making thus far. I have been saying that there is much evidence that feminism has been successful, my definition of that success here being that important steps have been taken around the globe in the direction of the full emancipation of women. Despite this evidence there is disgruntlement in many circles about the impact of the women's movement. In particular, feminists feel discouraged because: (a) there are obvious limits to the achievements won thus far, in terms of the breadth and depth of the changes wrought, particularly in class terms; (b) there are serious distortions in the way feminist ideas have been received by the culture at large; and (c) fears are held for the direction in which feminism is taking our society, as women reach for the options being held out to them and walk away—or so it appears—from their historical task of providing nurturance and support to others (especially children and men).

My points (b) and (c) are linked, I believe, in that some of the sense that feminist ideas have been distorted comes from the reality that only a part of the feminist programme for change has been found palatable— or even comprehensible—by the male-dominated power structures of our institutions. The part about *letting women in,* if I can express it this way, appears to have been grasped, however begrudgingly, in many areas of public life. But there is another part to feminism which is *letting women's values in*: this is the area where people balk, and understandably. The really revolutionary content of feminism has to do with the successful infusion of 'women-centred' values into patriarchal culture and politics.

In a lecture to Sydney feminists in 1983, the British journalist Beatrix Campbell discussed the political impact that was being felt in Great Britain as a result of the demonstrations by the women of Greenham Common against the installation of the American Cruise missiles. The initial reaction of the British press was enormous hostility and ridicule toward the women, who camped in winter and summer under sometimes gruelling conditions on the ground outside the barbed wire fencing surrounding the American military installation. Campbell charted a transformation in the attitude of the British press toward the women when they began to decorate the fence, as one of their gestures of protest, with all of the paraphernalia of British domestic life at its most sentimental.

The Greenham Common women wove bits of wool and cotton thread into the fence in an obvious cultural reference to Mary Daly's image of women as spinners and weavers, although I imagine that this kind of feminist allusion might have been lost on Fleet Street. But they also wove in dolls, and teddy bears, and children's toys. The net result of their artwork—a political piece of art if ever there was one!—was a highly successful evocation of childhood and woman's place. The fence became a statement of the power of nurturance and motherly love as a force against the destructive powers of the military, and it turned the press coverage around. Despite themselves, the hardnosed 'journos' found themselves moved by this association of domesticity with the struggle for world peace, and the coverage of the Greenham women became, for a time, most sympathetic to their cause.[16]

It is arguable, in this instance, that the Greenham Common women used the symbols of maternity and childhood to manipulate the press and that this was a cynical thing to do. But I believe that their actions had a deeper meaning and this is the point that Beatrix Campbell was making: the activist women in the Greenham Common action were symbolically transforming the public space of the missile installation into a domestic sphere writ large. They were bringing the values of their personal experience, including their socialisation as women to perform the role of mother, to bear on the political issue of war and militarism. This is the meaning of the teddy bears on the fence: they were making a statement of the need for maternal love, using what Sara Ruddick has termed maternal thinking[17] as a counterweight to the brutality and the nihilism implicit in the willingness to create, deploy and, ultimately, to explode nuclear weapons.

How do we get from a powerful but ephemeral symbolic statement of 'maternal' values as expressed by the women of Greenham Common to the effective integration of 'woman-centred values' into contemporary public life? How is it possible to place women's issues well and truly on the political agenda? I can only suggest some directions for this effort, which is under way in any case.

Firstly, the women who take up positions that involve as the chief focus of their duties the development and implementation of policies that will benefit women need to be self-conscious of the historical role they are in. This is particularly the case in Australia. Carol Johnson has written that 'the role of the state in bringing about social change for women is a particularly important issue in the country which invented the term "femocrat" '.[18] I have the impression that the femocrats in Australia are part of a unique and fleeting historical moment. The women entering public administration at senior levels (and I include myself in their number) are fresh-faced and naive. We are still able to say—as newcomers and outsiders—'What is this for; why do you have to do it this way?' Like a child learning to use a knife and fork for the first time, we are only learning and can still ask naive questions about the workings of a bureaucracy hitherto dominated by men and organised on behalf of male interests. Thus we act—but only, one presumes, for a limited period of time—as a critical, demanding, inquisitive presence. We should take full advantage of this to effect the changes that we seek, both in policy terms and in the way we carry out our daily business.

We should also take full advantage of our status as femocrats. To the extent that EEO officers, women's advisers and other such officials are selected on the basis of feminist commitment as a specific qualification for the position, we are in a privileged situation. Our political and social commitment to women's emancipation is part of what has earned us the right to work in these positions. This in turn creates an obligation on us to retain and to strengthen the feminist vision for which we were selected. I know that to say this in such broad terms begs a myriad of questions. It overlooks the thousand complications and conflicts that these jobs bring with them. I do not mean to minimise the difficulty and stress caused by the requirement to interpret a feminist vision in terms of narrow, specific and complex policy decisions. Nor am I underestimating the painfulness of engaging in a bureaucratic or political battle when one can find highly credentialed feminists firmly implanted on all three sides of any issue. But with these factors taken into account, I still believe that to be a femocrat is different from being a woman bureaucrat. One has been brought in not despite one's sex but in effect because of it. This should be, or at least it can be, a source of strength.

Secondly, the women's movement must continue to argue as it has done in the past that women's issues are everyone's issues. Childcare is not a problem for women but for parents and for society. A successful instance of this was the defeat of the consumption tax prior to the Tax Summit of 1985, brought about by an alliance of the welfare sector, the women's movement and the trade unions. This was an acknowledgement of a commonality of interests, rather than an isolation and 'ghettoisation' of feminist positions.[19]

Thirdly, feminists must acknowledge the links between the movement for the emancipation of women and other movements that seek to end oppression on the basis of race and class, however fraught with difficulties and ambiguities such alliances can be. At the 1986 conference in Canberra to consider items for the National Agenda for Women, Aboriginal women pleaded once again with the white women's movement (in the event, successfully) to link Aboriginal land rights to the rest of the agenda. Women from Greenham Common agreed to lend their support to the threatened Navajo and Hopi Native Americans who are being moved from their traditional homeland in northeastern Arizona, to facilitate the mining of coal and uranium.[20] The much vexed theoretical questions of how gender, class and race interact, and how the traditional socialist position of trade unions and political parties can and should accommodate the 'new' movements of women, environmentalists and indigenous people's movements, continue to fill the pages of socialist publications. A full and adequate theoretical account of these linkages—Marxism with feminism; feminism with Greens—and so on has still not seen the light of day. But in the interim perhaps the best way to work out these complex relationships is in the praxis of alliances around particular urgent political and social issues.

Finally, I return to my point about optimism and the standpoint of women. In the work to which I have already alluded, Sara Ruddick attempts to give a philosophical analysis of what she terms maternal thinking. She wants to isolate those features of maternal practice that give rise to a specific mode of thought. She is careful not to pin herself down to any particular biological interpretation, although she hedges her bets by pointing out that a great deal about the biological differences between the sexes remains unknown. But Ruddick emphasises that the characteristics she analyses have largely to do with the social role of raising children and are therefore transferable in principle to anyone, male or female, who carries out this responsibility. Ruddick's features of maternal thinking thus apply to the maternal as a social category.

Among the 'interests' that maternal thinking must satisfy, Ruddick lists: the preservation of life in the first instance, and then continually; the fostering of physical, emotional and intellectual growth, a process which, she says, accustoms the parent to a familiarity and ease with change which is expected (and therefore not threatening); the capacity to bring a quality of attention to others; and finally, most relevant to the argument I am making here, a form of resilience 'in the face of danger, disappointment, and unpredictability' that she terms 'clearsighted cheerfulness'. Ruddick writes:

> It is clear-sighted cheerfulness that Spinoza must have had in mind when he said: 'Cheerfulness is always a good thing and never excessive; it increases and assists the power of action.'[21]

Sheila Rowbotham has taken up my point about the need for a woman-centred vision for feminist action and has argued that, in moving toward the future we envisage, we cannot take a simple-minded interpretation as our guide. Not everything about the way women have been socialised in the past is useful for us in the future, nor is everything that has been symbolised by women's culture in the past necessarily progressive. We will have to pick and choose as we move forward.[22] I think it is an important point and I agree with her. Ruddick makes a similar point in saying that 'we must work to bring a *transformed* maternal thought into the public realm . . .'[23]

What I have tried to argue here is that in order to bring to fruition the changes we seek as feminists in our social and political life, one thing about the standpoint of women that is worth preserving and cultivating is our 'clearsighted cheerfulness', that is, our optimism. One way to put this into practice is to take account of the achievements of the women's movement as they occur and measure these not against the rest of what needs to be accomplished but against the strength of the obstacles overcome to date. Let us give ourselves proper credit and acknowledgement for feminist achievements, given the impermeability of the structures in need of transformation—from legislatures and courts to corporations, trade unions and bureaucracies of all kinds—and the strength of the forces arrayed against those who, in Sheila Rowbotham's phrase, search 'for a culture of equality and freedom'[24] for women alongside men.

8 Reconstructing the family

In the late twentieth century, a feminist commentary on the family has, I think, to commence from the premise that this is, in Jane Flax's expression, a contested terrain.[1] Who speaks 'for' the family? Who speaks 'against' it? In the crude picture of the world drawn for us by the media, feminists are anti-family by definition. I think that the reality is somewhat more complex. In the argument that I present here, I want to show that those who consider feminism to be the enemy of family life are half right. But if we concede that feminism, along with many other forces, is implicated in the current perceived crisis of the family, there are also elements in a feminist analysis of the family that are crucial to any positive rebuilding for the future.

In saying that the family is a contested terrain—conceptually, ideologically and politically—I am referring in particular to the use being made of the idea of the family by the New Right internationally. In the United States where the New Right has taken its most virulent form, linked as it is to apocalyptic religious fundamentalism, the ideologues of this political persuasion have tackled feminism head-on. The political campaigns of the New Right have been explicitly linked to a well-orchestrated appeal to nostalgia for the lost haven of the nuclear family with all of its traditional values.

The New Right ideology creates a stark polarisation between Good versus Evil. On the side of the angels is the traditional nuclear family with the nurturing mother at home raising her 2.1 children to believe in the traditional values, and the hardworking breadwinner father out there in the difficult but rewarding world of the paid workforce, bringing home the bacon. On the side of Satan and the forces of evil are the

This chapter was originally presented as a paper at the Second Australian Family Research Conference, convened by the Institute for Family Studies and held in Melbourne 26–28 November 1986.

lesbians, the homosexuals and the women in the paid workforce, all of whom—especially those holding down non-traditional jobs—are prey to (nonconjugal) sex, drugs and rock'n'roll. These persons are variously Communist-inspired and/or agents of the Iranian government (although since the Iran-Contra affair the vision of Iran as part of the Evil Empire appears to have faded somewhat).

The politics of this right-wing push have sexualised political discourse and political action in legal and illegal forms. As the political spectrum has shifted to the right, the right to abortion has taken a beating at the hands of the Supreme Court, as has the right to privacy in sexual behaviour with the re-criminalising of some sexual practices.[2] And there has been a concerted campaign of firebombing abortion clinics across the country.

This decision to take on the defence of family values is of course quite a deliberate political tactic. One of the chief strategists of the New Right in the United States, Richard Viguerie, has stated explicitly that the family is to the 1980s what Vietnam was to the 1960s and 1970s.[3] That is (I take him to mean), the family is the issue that divides people effectively by means of an emotional appeal that rallies them to the right of the political spectrum, in the manner that the war in Vietnam rallied people to the left during the anti-war movement.

It is easy to see this strategy of the New Right as some kind of a caricature, particularly in its exaggerated United States version. But it has been an effective tactic. Some feminists and their allies have sought in the American context to recuperate the lost ground politically by disavowing the accusation that it is feminists who have disrupted the family. Barbara Ehrenreich argues, for example, that the disintegration of traditional family structures is due more to changes in the degree of responsibility men were prepared to accept over the past thirty years than to feminist argument and activism. Others have sought to take the high ground by arguing that it is the Left that truly supports the values of family life. A bitter debate has in fact erupted over this tactic, as it entails a disavowal by some left theorists of the right to abortion.[4]

I propose to take a different tack, and argue that feminism has, indeed, played a role in what is widely being perceived as the disintegration of family life. In order to defend this proposition, however, I must make it clear that I want to use the word 'disintegration' at a number of different levels. I think that feminist theory and practice have disintegrated the family, that is, deconstructed and disaggregated it, in at least three ways: analytically; politically; and ideologically.

First, analytically: if we ask the question, how does feminist theory 'see' the family, the answer is that in reality it does not look at the family directly, as an entity. Rather, it has tended to break up the idea of the family into a number of component parts, looking at each of these parts from a female perspective and, more specifically, from the perspective of women's experiences and interests. Some of the components are, in the first instance, the complex of issues around love and marriage; childbearing in relation to reproductive control; sexuality and women's freedom to express this, as opposed to the violent control of rape; the economic dependence of wives with no income outside the home versus the relative independence of women working for wages; sex role or gender identity construction and the role of the family in their reproduction; and so on. In short, one can argue that feminist analysis of the family has been a process of fragmentation, of taking The Family apart and dissecting it into those elements that have been seen as making it an oppressive arena for women.

Secondly, feminist analysis of the family has tended to reject the analytical framework that dichotomises sex and family life from paid work into 'private' and 'public' spheres, and conceives of the family as a domain separate from the rest of social and political life. Instead, feminist writers have sought to find a way of analysing families as part of a system that organises the functions that the family performs in relation to society as a whole.

Juliet Mitchell's formulation of this is well known. She looks at women's role from the point of view of four 'structures': production, reproduction, sexuality and the socialisation of children. Similarly Rayna Rapp, Ellen Ross and Renate Bridenthal have drawn on the insights of family history to isolate the elements of kinship, household and consumption, which characterise the functions of families over time, with their size and criteria for inclusion or exclusion varying by class, ethnicity and historical period.[5] Jane Flax characterises the family in yet another way, as the point of 'intersection' for 'three primary forms of social relations', namely, the production of environments for survival (I think these are houses), reproduction (of children) and psychodynamics.[6]

The much-cited formulation by Gayle Rubin of the 'sex-gender system' similarly seeks to place family relations into a broad scheme by which society organises the social relations of sexuality.[7] In all of this, feminist analysis is trying to show that the family has certain particular functions. We look to the family for intimacy; for nurturance; in order to reproduce ourselves; and in order to construct and reconstruct the gender identity of the next generation. But none of this takes place in isolation from the rest of society.

Thus in feminist analysis the family is not one thing, nor is it an isolated thing. It is a set of relations and functions that have to be analysed critically from the point of view of their effects on women and the options offered to women within these. The feminist view of the family is not all one-sidedly critical. In recent years, for example, there has been a considerable attempt to 'recuperate' motherhood as a feminist activity. The writings of Nancy Chodorow, Adrienne Rich, Sara Ruddick and others have looked at mothering as a source of enrichment and creativity for women.[8] But these analyses place mothering in a social context and point to the lack of freedom of this activity when it is constrained by the lack of reproductive choice and by the requirements of rigid gender expectations.

In its concern to link the family to larger social structures and broader social objectives, feminism is, of course, in a respectable line of descent. Much social theory of the past two centuries has concerned itself with utopian visions of alternative societies. Some of the social experiments of the early nineteenth century, like some of these in the heady 1960s within our own experience, sought to remodel society at the micro level by experimenting with alternative family forms. One thinks of the Fourierists, for example. There is a long tradition, too, of linking the structures that characterise family life with those that govern public life. Hence the debate among the members of the Frankfurt school about the origins of the authoritarian personality. If the ills of society could be traced to the structure of character, so that people conformed to the requirements of the state (to the point of accepting and even embracing the state violence of Nazism), then it was a fair enough argument that change had to come at the micro level in the structures of family life that shaped character from the moment of birth.[9]

Feminism inherits this tradition with of course the added twist of commencing the analysis from a woman's point of view, and more particularly from the point of view of the mother. The writings of Dorothy Dinnerstein and Jane Flax,[10] and those of Chodorow, Rich and Ruddick already cited, among others, have sought to trace the origins of misogyny as a fact of social life. If, from a feminist point of view, the hatred of women is the fundamental problem to be explained and then eliminated, then in the first instance one needs to find out its source. Hypothetically this can be traced to the original power of the mother over the helpless infant, in a world where the power of the father is experienced at a later, less threatening stage of development.

All of this takes us deep into the land of psychoanalysis and the debates over Freud and the post-Freudians.[11] It also leads us down the path of the social construction of gender, the family as the birthplace of both masculine and feminine character structures. It is the construction of masculinity, in particular, within the family that feminists associate with a destructive emotional stance that underlies patriarchal state power in the post-nuclear age. This is the cluster of ideas behind the women's peace movement as expressed in the encampments at Greenham Common, Seneca Falls, at Parliament House in Canberra by 'Women for Survival' and other places around the globe.

The 'Women for Survival' branch of feminism is connected to, but should not, I think, be conflated with, other strands of feminist utopianism which draw a landscape in which the damaging effects of maleness can be removed at the stroke of a pen. One thinks of Monique Wittig's *Les Guérillières*, or, last century, of Charlotte Perkin Gilman's *Herland*, a society where only women live and where aggression and violence (in Perkins' version) have been removed. (Wittig's utopia, in sharp contrast, paints women as Warrior Amazons.[12]) This, too, is the direction of radical feminist separatism as described in the work of Mary Daly.[13] The problems of male character structure and male hatred of women can be excised by imagining a world where maleness, the preoccupations of men and their power over women can all be wiped from the canvas. In some versions of feminism, then, the issues raised by the oppressive social relations of the family are dealt with by abolishing the family—and indeed male-female relationships—altogether.

Thirdly, and perhaps most crucially from the point of view of the argument that I am making here, feminist analysis disaggregates the family into its component parts or players in order to ask significant questions about power and resources. It is common to recall the slogan 'the personal is the political' as one of the hallmark insights of the women's liberation movement of the 1960s. I have written elsewhere on the important links that existed between the theoretical framework of radical feminism in its 1960s versions and that of the New Left against which feminists were rebelling.[14] Most particularly it is noteworthy in this context that the analysis of interpersonal power dynamics underlying the writing of Anne Koedt, Shulamith Firestone, Ti-Grace Atkinson, Robin Morgan and others had close ties to the analysis proposed by members of the radical psychology movement, most notably R.D. Laing.

Laing was concerned to demystify family life, as well as the madness/ sanity dichotomy of orthodox psychiatry, by looking at what he called 'the politics of the family'. This kind of analysis deromanticised the relationship of parent to child, substituting for the concept of love a more cold-blooded picture of coercive behaviour. Ultimately, in the Laing model, parents produced schizophrenia in their children who were seeking on the one hand to remain their authentic selves and, on the other, to meet the straitjacketing requirements of parental expectations in terms of both behaviour and affect.[15]

The Laing tradition of radical psychology was, I believe, an important source of the radical feminist analysis which saw male-female relationships within marriage as fundamentally based upon an imbalance of power. Like the politics of the family, sexual politics within the heterosexual couple was disguised by the concept of love, with its elaborate ideology of romance, sharply deconstructed by Firestone in her commentary on the meaning of 'falling in love'. That there was a micropolitics of interpersonal power between men and women became a founding assumption of radical feminism, underlying the subsequent analysis of issues such as rape, child sexual assault and wife-battering. The economic implications of this analysis led to the examination of the distribution of resources between husband and wife of the kind investigated in the work of Meredith Edwards.[16] And of course in this context the access of wives to independent income through re-entry into education and jobs was seen, in a feminist framework, as part of the necessary process of redressing the imbalance of power in domestic life.

If feminist theory in its many varieties disintegrated—that is, disaggregated and deconstructed—the family analytically, feminist practice has certainly undermined the family politically, if we define the family here in its most traditional patriarchal interpretation. I certainly do not wish to argue here that all wings and branches of the women's movement in the United States, Australia and elsewhere have deliberately set out to attack the family as a social structure. But it is undeniable that the focus of feminist activism has been upon actions to enhance the power of women, both within their 'private' relationships and in their relationships to 'public' life.

A brief listing of feminist initiatives and campaigns over the past two decades or so, separated into these two categories, serves to illustrate the point.

Reforms affecting women in their relation to 'private' life, that is, in personal relations to self, men, children and other women

- changes to laws governing rape, including rape in marriage

- establishment of women's refuges

- access to abortion and safe contraception

- access to increased information about health care

- campaigns against unnecessary surgery (hysterectomies; breast removals)

- childcare

- payments to supporting mothers

- reforms to family law easing divorce restrictions

- reform of laws on homosexuality
- consciousness-raising groups
- establishment of feminist forms of psychotherapy

Reforms affecting women in their relation to 'public' life, that is, the paid workforce and cultural and political institutions

- establishment of Women's Studies courses
- entry of mature-age women to university
- affirmative action and EEO measures to increase job opportunities at senior levels and to open up non-traditional areas of work
- campaign for equal pay
- campaign against sexual harassment
- campaign against pornography
- women's peace movement
- women candidates for parliament, party office, trade union executive
- establishment of feminist journals, publishing houses, film collectives
- campaign to bring 'women's issues' such as repetitive strain injury (RSI) onto the agenda of trade union activism

The categorisation of 'private' and 'public' in the context of feminism is, as is obvious from the list, immediately suspect, as I have noted already. For example, childcare becomes relevant to women as they seek to enter the paid workforce; yet it is a 'private' matter in relation to patterns of childrearing. The point I wish to make here, however, is that the focus of women's movement activism inevitably has been upon a series of actions that increase the social power of women as a group. This has been premised upon an analysis that sees women as being at the mercy of the power of men unless they can obtain sufficient education, control over their reproductive lives, income, and support to gain some independence and autonomy in the direction of their own lives. While this does not in any way rule out of court the decisions of many women to enter into and indeed remain in relations of traditional family life, it is a set of objectives that runs well and truly counter to the 'barefoot and pregnant' model of the woman locked into the confines of the traditional patriarchal family.

As I argue elsewhere in this book, it is a matter for debate as to how widespread and effective feminist campaigns have been, and how in particular the outcomes of the campaigns, in terms of legislative reform, have benefitted the women for whose sake they were undertaken. But there can be no doubt that for some considerable proportion of women the influence of feminist activism has been to broaden their options for education and employment and therefore to redefine their relationship to their families and their roles within these.

There is, finally, a third sense in which feminism has helped to disintegrate the family, and that is ideologically. By this I mean that feminist perspectives, writings and campaigns have raised public consciousness about a number of realities that were in previous times covered with a veil of romantic beliefs. The case I am making here can perhaps be envisaged most clearly by means of a set of contrasts between the myth of the family that most of us hold dear and the social realities that we have had to begin to confront, however painful this exercise might be.

The myth in our minds about childhood is of a safe fantasy world inhabited by characters like Peter Rabbit. The reality we are looking at is the widespread incidence of incest and of child abuse in general. The myth about marriage conjures up a vision of sexual fidelity and loyalty and of married love enduring forever and a day. The reality we confront includes a sharp rise in the rate of divorce, rape in marriage (until recently sanctioned by law everywhere), wife-battering (now sanitised in the expression 'domestic violence'), and the phenomenon of married men contracting AIDS outside the conjugal bedroom. The myth of motherhood connotes unconditional motherly love and acceptance. The reality reveals the psychological and economic crisis for many women constituted by childbirth: postpartum depression, interpretable in some instances as rage (the Australian national obsession with the fate of Azaria Chamberlain is suggestive in this context, as Judith Allen has pointed out[17]); and the stress of acquiring new mouths to feed in an era of declining economic support. Finally, the myth suggests to us that the children will grow up to follow in Dad's and Mum's footsteps. The reality is, instead, a generation plagued with teenage joblessness, drug abuse and existential despair, faced with the uncertainty of a future altogether in the post-nuclear era.[18]

Some of the anger directed toward feminists, in this context, has a 'shoot the messenger' quality. In many cases it has been feminists who have begun to articulate the social truths that many of us might have preferred not to know. It is not of course the case that feminism as a set of beliefs has caused the disintegration evoked by this account. Rather, it is feminism that has pointed to the reality behind the myth, and it is easier to be angry at the truth-teller than to cope with the truth.

There are, then, two or three layers of the onion to peel away here, two or three levels of meaning. First, I have argued that feminism as a set of beliefs and as an analysis, in its many varieties, inevitably disaggregates the idea of the family into a set of structures that it sees as oppressive to women. Secondly, feminism as a social influence is, indeed, partly responsible for some of the recent stresses on family life. The newly won independence of some women and the changes they have made in their lives have caused disturbance and upset to to their families (parental and/or marital). Thirdly, feminist analysis is upsetting because it lays bare some features about family life that most of us have trouble thinking about, namely, the realities of rape, incest, child abuse, wife battering and other practices that jar our comfortable associations with home and hearth.

It would however be both unjust and ahistorical to contend that feminism—viewed either as a set of analytical tools or as a social and political movement—can have had in itself the power to bring about the changes we are experiencing in our social life. It would probably be more accurate to say that feminism has been as much an effect as a cause. The changes themselves have their roots in major historical shifts: in the composition of the economy, particularly the move away from manufacturing to services, with the effects this has had on women's labour force participation; the sharp rise in unemployment of recent years; the impact of the 1960s and the cultural and social revolution that accompanied the civil rights and anti-war agitation of those years; and many other factors.

I have argued elsewhere that some of the current anger against feminism and feminists stems from a perception that the women's movement has encouraged women to give away their role of nurturing service to others and instead to seek their entitlements as equal members of society (see 'The Case for Feminist Optimism', page 79 and ff). The industrial struggle of nurses for equitable conditions may perhaps be seen as a metaphor for this transformation in the role of women. But the argument I am putting here is that there are vast social changes that go far beyond the women's revolution that we are all having trouble coping with.

It is therefore unrealistic for political figures of whatever persuasion to argue that we should turn the clock back and seek to live again in the 1950s (or the 1850s, for that matter). One cannot reverse the direction of social history. It would be more constructive, in my view, to ask in what ways can we use the insights of feminist analysis to strengthen, not perhaps the Family as the imaginary reified entity that seems so elusive, but those elements of human life that we look to the family to provide? In the space remaining I suggest some principles that might guide us in this effort.

First, I have indicated that feminist analysis looks at the family (in a neo-functionalist way, perhaps) as a site in which certain needs are met: for intimacy, for nurturance and for reproduction. This suggests that in debates about the family we ought perhaps to focus less upon form than upon substance. Instead of asking whether households still have the traditional form of the nuclear family, we ought to be asking if the arrangements of the household meet the needs of those within it for nurturance, intimacy and reproduction, no matter who inhabits the household and what their exact kinship relations are to one another? We should, in short, be more flexible in our definition of what constitutes a proper family and make room, instead, for a variety of forms and permutations. This makes space, for example, for alternative family structures favoured by some Aborigines and some people from non-Anglo Saxon backgrounds. It also makes space for households based on a kinship of affinity rather than of blood, and makes room for homosexual and lesbian couples as well as for heterosexuals. This allows us to accept the legitimacy of a range of household arrangements and in effect sanctions an expanded and flexible definition of what constitutes a family group.

Second, feminist analysis invariably contests the fictive boundary between public and private spheres, pointing out instead that public policy shapes and constrains private life, in the interest of encouraging some kinds of outcomes and discouraging others. The family sphere is well and truly shaped by public policy by means of a variety of measures, from education and tax policy to direct family supports of various kinds. In addition, issues that in the past were considered private to families have become and will increasingly become public issues, in part because the insistence of feminist activists has put them on the political agenda. The debates over maintenance and welfare payments, over wife-battering and over childcare illustrate this point. In the light of this, Eva Cox has argued that the debate over child abuse is wrongly framed when it seeks to create a model of 'normal' and 'deviant' families. In her view, this takes things by the wrong end in that it argues that only deviant or failing families require support. Rather, she thinks that we ought to assume that everyone who is raising children requires and deserves social support. That is, the raising of children is a matter of public concern and public responsibility.[19]

The need for support extends to structures of all kinds that serve as sites for the establishment of intimacy and nurturance. As Linda Gordon notes in the United States context,

> the women's movement has already done a great deal toward building supportive institutions that prefigure a better society: day-care centers, shelters, women's centers, communes, gay bars and bars where women feel comfortable, publications, women's studies programs and health clinics.[20]

The nearly intolerable pressure on private relationships to provide all possible nurturance grows, as Jane Flax has noted, from an organisation of public life that precludes these kinds of supportive relationships from flourishing. The women's movement has tried, with some success, to even the balance somewhat.

Finally, feminist analysis insists on seeing things from a woman's point of view. If indeed the structure of the nuclear family meets the needs of most people, then the way to ensure its survival is to provide the kind of network of support, financial and otherwise, that will enable it to flourish. If it is a minority preference, then well and good: society ought to be able to tolerate a hundred flowers, a myriad of arrangements that satisfy people's needs for intimacy, nurturance and reproduction. The one thing in all of this that ought to be non-negotiable, from a feminist point of view, is the requirement that women retain the ground that they have won for their own decision making, for choosing their own path in life. If the traditional patriarchal nuclear family is incompatible with this objective, then perhaps we ought to let it quietly expire.

9 Gender as a category of analysis

In this chapter, I want to explore the state of play in the use of the concept of gender as a category of analysis. In its current form, gender re-entered academic discourses as the result (direct or indirect) of feminist activism. But many are now expressing doubts as to the usefulness of the term altogether. Elizabeth Spelman argues that the word contains within itself the seeds of racism. Its use immediately connotes 'white women', and thus it automatically fails in its mission of conveying the notion of 'all women' that it was designed to signify.[1] And Denise Thompson has urged that we give up on using the sex/gender distinction altogether.[2]

Surely the dissatisfaction with the use of the term is related to what has become of it in academic settings and, in particular, to the failure of the word itself to continue carrying the political urgency of its activist origins. But this is related to a larger question and that is, what directions has feminist scholarship taken since its arrival into relative respectability in university life? Upon my re-entry to the world of Women's Studies in the United States, I was struck by a number of changes that have raised questions in my mind. Has the price of relative success in the academy been a certain kind of absorption and transformation, a taming as it were? I keep getting the sense of a lack of fit between feminist theory in its many complex academic varieties, with the lived experience of women in a period of moving and miraculous transformation for some women and of increasing oppression and violence for others.[3]

It is in this context that I want to address some issues in the current

Previous versions of this chapter were presented in whole or in part at the Department of Anthropology and Sociology, Monash University, Melbourne (August 1988); the Women's Studies Program, the University of California at Davis (November 1988); the Graduate Group for Feminist Studies, State University of New York, Buffalo (February 1989); and the Department of Sociology, Yale University (March 1989).

debate about gender as a category of analysis. I will be looking at three different texts, each of which speaks about gender in a different way. I want to use these as examples, by way of raising some questions of how we can usefully go forward in social analysis in speaking and thinking about gender.

The texts I will be using are: Catharine A. MacKinnon, *Feminism Unmodified*; Teresa de Lauretis, 'The Technology of Gender'; and Aihwa Ong, *Spirits of Resistance and Capitalist Discipline: Factory Women in Malaysia*. These texts come, respectively, from the disciplines of law, literary and film criticism and anthropology. Two are based in the experience of First World women; the third draws on an experience of Third World women (if one can still use this term). Before turning to the texts, let me sketch in some necessary background.

The resurgence of the women's movement in the 1960s had important repercussions within the academy, especially in the United States. One result was a searching examination of the 'human sciences', as the French call them, for the impact of male or patriarchal biases on all aspects of academic work, from basic issues of methodology to findings about social life. This enterprise has now been carried on for nearly two decades and there are very few areas which have escaped what most would, I suspect, consider to be a very fruitful, if not always a very comfortable, exercise in self-examination.[4]

One of the central results of this interaction between feminism and academic inquiry has been the focus upon gender. It is nearly a cliché of academic writing in some circles to draw the parallel between the impact of Marxism on social thought in the nineteenth century, imposing on intellectuals a concern with class as an analytical category, and the impact of feminism in the twentieth century, similarly imposing a concern with gender. The 'discovery' of gender and its incorporation into social theory has created a new literature and marked out some extremely fruitful lines of enquiry. But of course feminism is not just about carving out a new set of research problems. It is also an analysis of a system of oppression and (in most versions) a blueprint for fundamental social change.

The intervention of feminism into the academy, like that of Marxism, is therefore highly political in nature. It is not an inquiry for the sake of inquiry alone, but it is also an endeavour that seeks to 'dismantle the master's house', in the words of Audre Lorde. My standpoint here is of someone who commences from the premise that the university as an institution, in its several roles, is *a priori* a political enterprise in the broadest sense, and the site, like other social institutions, of various kinds of struggles. That is, I do not wish to be misunderstood as arguing that feminism and Marxism politicised what was otherwise an ivory tower of value-free inquiry. It is therefore a matter of some considerable urgency to look carefully at the debates on gender. How does this concept get used in academic language and research? There is a politics surrounding the concept of gender, in my view, and we would do well to be aware of how this gets played out.

But the situation is more complicated than this. From the beginning of the second wave of the women's movement, a central point of debate within American feminist theory and practice was over the issue of difference.[5] To summarise this very briefly: one strand of feminist theory commenced from the premise laid down by Simone de Beauvoir that the oppression of women stemmed from their differences from men: their biological functions and the social responsibilities and constraints deriving from these; and the psychological and social adaptations required of girls to become women (in her famous formulation, 'One is not born but becomes a woman.') De Beauvoir can be seen as the founder of a direct lineage through Betty Friedan to Germaine Greer and Kate Millett, and from these to Martina Navratilova and Steffi Graf.

This is a shorthand way of saying that the path to liberation lay through the elimination of biological and social differences between men and women to the extent possible. In social policy terms this meant the removal of barriers — legal; economic; and psychosocial — and thereby the opening of the public world to women. In the broadest terms, difference meant oppression, and the objective, then, was sameness or androgyny. Another way to express this is to use the concept of symmetry: one sought, to the extent possible, to create a world in which the lives and the life chances of men and women were symmetrical, rather than lying at opposite ends of a spectrum of difference.

The theoretical basis of this position, from the point of view of the social sciences, was drawn from the theory of sex-role socialisation. Second wave feminist theorists relied heavily on the work of Mirra Komarovsky and other writers who turned Talcott Parsons on his head and argued that the socially appropriate roles of instrumental/rational for men and affective/emotional for women had outlived their usefulness. In the late twentieth century, this was no longer an adequate preparation for social life. But because these roles had been socially organised, they could be socially transformed, once the critique had been broadly accepted. The agencies of socialisation had only to rewrite their programmes, so to speak, and to provide both men and women with a broad range of common skills and passions. How far such a new set of programmes could be carried was then debated, and continues to be debated, both in academic circles and elsewhere, with sociobiologists taking up the terrain of a conservative position, setting out the limits, as it were, to the reprogramming of the sexes, and therefore, of the species.

Meanwhile, of course, there was another strand of feminist theory, which I and other writers have called a 'woman-centred perspective'. These theorists — Mary Daly, Jean Baker Miller, Susan Griffin and

Andrea Dworkin, among others (and to these one could add some of the French feminist theorists such as Hélène Cixous and Luce Irigaray) — sought to argue for the instrinsic worth of women's differences as a source of moral and political values. To these writers the goal was not to diminish female difference but, on the contrary, to celebrate it.

The feminist theory of women's difference now occupies a complex terrain, difficult to trace as it extends to many different points of the compass. There is neither space nor time to do a full history of the evolution of this idea which tries to turn Simone de Beauvoir on *her* head and argue that it is women's difference that is a source of richness and creativity, without falling into the historical and political trap of seeing the difference as biologically determined (this is usually referred to in shorthand as the danger of essentialism).[6] The celebration of difference, for example, finds its way into literary theory in the extensive debate over whether or not one can speak of women's language or writing. It is also linked to the philosophical work that attacks the entire tradition of Western epistemology as being based upon dualisms and dichotomies, of which masculine/feminine is a fundamental paradigm, and which seeks to deconstruct this tradition using a concept of difference that appears to rejoin the feminist project.[7] The strand of difference also runs through the controversial work of Carol Gilligan on women's moral development.[8]

The two tendencies of feminism coexist today in a complex field of forces. Within the international women's movement, there is now a vigorous debate about the way forward. There is widespread dissatisfaction with the model of seeking to eliminate difference, often derided and dismissed as merely 'bourgeois' feminism. But there is equal difficulty with the model of celebrating difference, which in some versions appears to be a path toward the retreat from struggle.

I believe that one can see echoes of the sameness/difference debate in many different arenas.[9] For example, one might cite the debate internationally over the use of the law in the service of feminist objectives. In the American context, this takes the form of the critique of the doctrine of equal rights, which has come to be seen as a kind of straitjacket rather than a vehicle for the defence of the special needs and requirements of women. The *locus classicus* of this is the argument over whether pregnancy should be seen as a condition that is unique to women or as a disability, like others incurred by men and women, that can be compensated for using medical insurance.[10]

A similar issue informs the debate over which is the superior strategy, affirmative action or equal pay for work of comparable value. Should we seek equality of opportunity for women in the workplace via, in effect, eliminating the sexual division of labour, by breaking down the barriers to women's access at all levels of traditionally male areas of work? Or is it better to leave the sexual division of labour in place, but to make women's work economically viable by means of a comparable worth strategy?[11]

In the academy, the sameness/difference issue plays itself out in the longstanding debate over the establishment of Women's Studies programmes. Should they be designed to be structurally distinct from the rest of the university, with their own budgets, curriculum and staff? Or should one attempt to infuse Women's Studies materials into all aspects of the curriculum to avoid the dangers of ghettoisation and marginalising of feminist perspectives? (The use of curriculum integration programmes begins to answer this question; it is a way, in effect, of doing both.)

There is, then, a lack of clarity and consensus among feminist activists and scholars in many areas as to which is the way forward, from a theoretical as well as from a social policy point of view.[12] But the question over which is the way forward is intimately linked to another question, which is this: what exactly is it that we as feminists are up against? How does the sex/gender system actually operate? Can one effectively intervene in the system, to make it, somehow, fairer? I can only allude here to the extensive debate among feminists of many persuasions about the concept of patriarchy and how it intersects with the class system of capitalism.[13] There are echoes, here, of the twentieth-century attempt to explain the persistence of capitalist culture in the face of its manifest embodiment of systems of exploitation. In effect, the debate over a theory of gender is a new debate over hegemony, translated from the world of class analysis into the world of the sex/gender system. As Bob Connell has noted,

> it was often suggested in the early 1970s that sex roles were 'artificial' because they were socially created (by media, schools or whatever). There was a sense that if you poked a finger at them it would go right through. Since then a good many fingers have been poked and they did not go through.[14]

The debate over the way forward is complicated by the difficulty of getting a handle on what works and what doesn't. But it is also complicated by the play of forces when gender and the politics of gender are part of what is at stake. We are in the midst of a period of social change in which gender issues have been profoundly politicised around the world — or perhaps a better word here would be contested — and in which feminist women, and non-feminist women as well, are plunged into an arena in which we ourselves, our identities, our self-definitions, are part of the struggle. The experience of women (and men) on the front lines of the gender wars is complex and varied, and is only beginning to be documented.

Various writers have tried to get a handle on this set of issues, using expressions like 'gender experience' (my preference) or 'gendered experiences' (Martha Fineman) or 'the experience of gender' (Teresa de Lauretis).[15] When I talk about this, I am casting my net very wide. I refer, for example, to the phenomenon of the first woman 'X': firefighter; law professor; construction worker; and university president or vice-chancellor. And I am also referring to the activists who are framing new kinds of legislation (for example, establishing that sexual harassment is a detriment under the law), and who are attempting to give structural and legal form and shape to some of the claims of feminism.

However the shaping and reshaping of gender identity goes on in a whole range of areas, not only those directly affected by the work of activists. The concept of gender is also affected by what happens in these other arenas, as we will see in the work of Aihwa Ong on Malaysian factory workers. It is in this context of fluidity and conflict that the concept of gender, and a proper theory of gender, are struggling to be born.

Let me now turn to my three texts and see what light these shed on the notion of what we mean by gender as a social category. *Feminism Unmodified*, by Catharine MacKinnon, is a series of talks that she has given since she published her two now famous articles in *Signs* which attempted to establish the argument that sex is to feminism as class is to Marxism. The essays in this volume are more accessible and possibly less controversial, although nothing MacKinnon does really escapes controversy.[16] I want to focus here on some of what MacKinnon says on gender, as I believe that her comments on this represent a kind of bottom line for the discussion of the concept.

I will start by quoting MacKinnon on the difference (sic) between liberal and radical feminisms. This material is drawn from her 1982 piece on 'Women, Self-Possession and Sport'. MacKinnon is commenting here on the attempts of women to receive equal treatment with men in the areas of training, funding and access to sporting facilities, as well as on their highly successful efforts to break out of the stereotyped expectations of what women can and cannot achieve physically (the paradigm case here is women running the marathon). In a liberal feminist approach, MacKinnon writes:

> the problem of the inequality of sexes revolves around gender
> differentiation. The view is that there are real differences between the
> sexes, usually biological or natural. Upon these differences, society has
> created some distorted, inaccurate, irrational, and arbitrary distinctions;
> sex stereotypes or sex roles. To eliminate sex inequality, in this view, is to
> eliminate these wrong and irrational distinctions ... The solution that
> responds to this diagnosis is that we need to ignore or eliminate these
> distortions so that people can realise their potential as individuals ...
> (pp. 117-18)

In contrast, a radical feminist perspective argues that it is doubtful that

> differences or differentiation have much to do with inequality. Sexism is a
> problem not of gender differentiation, but of gender hierarchy, in which
> gender differentiation is only one strategy ... the problem is ... male
> supremacy and female subjection.

This distinction is particularly relevant in discussions of women and
sport.

> From this second point of view, issues like rape, incest, sexual harassment,
> prostitution, pornography — issues of the violation of women, in
> particular of women's sexuality — connect directly with issues of athletics.
> The systematic maiming of women's physicality that marks those athletic
> and physical pursuits that women have been forced or pressured or
> encouraged to do, on the one hand, connect with those we have been
> excluded from doing, on the other. If you ask, not why do women and
> men do different physical activities, but why has femininity *meant* physical
> weakness, you notice that someone who is physically weak is more easily
> able to be raped, available to be molested, open to sexual harassment.
> Feminine means violable. (p. 118)

In other words, gender is not, in MacKinnon's view, fundamentally
about difference. It is about power. And, as she argues, to talk about
differences as though these were the cause or root of the problem is, in
her mind, a kind of refusal to see the point of feminism, or indeed, a
form of opposition to feminism.

> Gender is an inequality of power, a social status based on who is
> permitted to do what to whom. Only derivatively is it a difference ...
> Inequality comes first; differences come after. Inequality is substantive and
> identifies a disparity; difference is abstract and falsely symmetrical. If this is
> so, a discourse of gender difference serves as ideology to neutralise,
> rationalise, and cover disparities of power, even as it appears to criticise
> them. Difference is the velvet glove on the iron fist of domination ... One
> of the most deceptive antifeminisms in society, scholarship, politics and
> law is the persistent treatment of gender as if it truly is a question of
> difference, rather than treating the gender difference as a construct of the
> difference gender makes. (pp. 8–9)

MacKinnon makes the same point, slightly more forcefully, in an essay
on 'Desire and Power', originally a talk in the context of a discussion
of social theory, including speakers on deconstruction and
poststructuralism.

> Gender here is a matter of dominance, not difference. Feminists have
> noticed that women and men are equally different but not equally
> powerful. Explaining the subordination of women to men, a political
> condition, has nothing to do with difference in any fundamental sense.
> Consequentially, it has a *lot* to do with difference, because the ideology of
> difference has been so central in its enforcement. Another way to say that

is, there would be no such thing as what we know as the sex difference — much less would it be the social issue it is or have the social meaning it has — were it not for male dominance. Sometimes people ask me, 'Does that mean you think there's no difference between women and men?' The only way I know how to answer that is: of course there is; the difference is that men have power and women do not. (p. 51)

Are sex differences, then, totally irrelevant to the concept of gender? Of course not, says MacKinnon. Precisely because of their linkage to power, the meaning of difference is deeply internalised. MacKinnon's discussion of women in sport makes this process clear, and speaks, by the way, to the issue of how the social structures of gender 'interface' with the subjective consciousness of the individual — a matter Bob Connell wrestles with in his book on gender and power.[17]

> The notion that women cannot do certain things, cannot break certain records, cannot engage in certain physical pursuits has been part of preventing women from doing those things. It isn't only that women are excluded, it's that even women who do sport are limited. This isn't just ideas or images — or just women, for that matter. When you think, for instance, about the relationship between the scientific discovery of the physical possibility of running a mile in less than x time and people actually running the mile in less than x time, you see a real relationship beween images of the possibility of a particular achievement and the actual physical ability to do it. Anyone who trains seriously understands this on some level.

The objectification of women has physical consequences for the relative power positions of women and men.

> What I'm suggesting is that the sexual, by which I mean the gender, objectification of women that has distinguished between women, on the one hand, and the successful athlete, on the other, has reached deeper than just mistaken ideas about what women can and cannot do, notions that can be thought out of existence by the insightful or the exceptionally ambitious. It is not only ideas in the head that have excluded us from resources and most everything else. It is also the social meaning of female identity that has restricted and contained us. If a woman is defined hierarchically so that the male idea of a woman defines womanhood, and if men have power, this idea becomes reality. It is therefore real. It is not just an illusion or a fantasy or a mistake. It becomes *embodied* because it is enforced. (pp. 118–19)

For MacKinnon, then, the conflation of 'gender' with 'difference' is a means of covering up, stifling, silencing the real message of feminism, which is a global confrontation with male dominance, and with the violent outcomes of the system of male dominance for the women who are its victims. Discussions of gender difference, then, soften and mute the impact of feminism 'unmodified', by which she means, not socialist, not Marxist, not liberal, but feminism *tout court*. As she puts it, with characteristic passion, 'If it does not track bloody footprints across your desk, it is probably not about women.' (p. 9)

To summarise her position, then, broadly, for MacKinnon, the central issue in discussing gender is the unequal distribution of power between men and women and the consequent subordination of women to men. For Teresa de Lauretis, the central issue is the need to find a route between the Scylla of androgyny and the Charybdis of idealised female difference into the open sea of freedom from gender. Her experience of the constraints of gender has taught her its reality. It is, she indicates, a fantasy to imagine that we can simply argue, think and/or act our way out of a system of gender that controls us. On the one hand she cannot participate in an idealised notion of an essential female set of qualities that define and separate women from men.

> I find it impossible to share some women's belief in a matriarchal past or a contemporary 'matristic' realm presided over by the Goddess, a realm of female tradition, marginal and subterranean and yet all positive and good, peace-loving, ecologically correct, matrilineal, matrifocal, non-Indo-European, and so forth; in short, a world untouched by ideology, class and racial struggle, television — a world untroubled by the contradictory demands and oppressive rewards of gender as I, and surely those women, too, have daily experienced it.

But

> on the other hand, and much for the same reasons, I find it equally impossible to dismiss gender either as an essentialist and mythical idea of the kind I have just described, or as the liberal-bourgeois idea encouraged by media advertisers; someday soon, somehow, women will have careers, their own last names and property, children, husbands, and/or female lovers according to preference — and all of that without altering the existing social relations and the heterosexual structures to which our society, and most others, are securely screwed. (pp. 20–21)

De Lauretis draws on Foucault's concept of the technology of sex to point out that there are technologies of gender that shape and reshape us in their image, and that these include some of the very work, including that by feminist academics, that is seeking to free everyone, but especially women, from the constraints of gender.

> The construction of gender goes on as busily today as it did in earlier times, say the Victorian era. And it goes on not only where one might expect it to — in the media, the private and public schools, the courts, the family, nuclear or extended or single-parented — in short, in what Louis Althusser has called the 'ideological state apparati.' The construction of gender also goes on, if less obviously, in the academy, in the intellectual community, in avant-garde artistic practices and radical theories, even, and indeed especially, in feminism. (p. 3)

De Lauretis is particularly scathing toward social theorists who purport to be taking account of women and women's experience, but who instead establish or rather re-establish an archetypal Woman who has nothing to do with the actual lived experience of women themselves. I alluded early to the work of Alice Jardine on this point. De Lauretis cites the work of Rosi Braidotti, the philosopher, as follows.

> In her analysis of the notion of femininity in contemporary French philosophy, Rosi Braidotti sees that notion as central to its foremost preoccupations: the critique of rationality, the demystification of unified subjectivity (the individual as subject of knowledge), and the investigation of the complicity between knowledge and power. The radical critique of subjectivity, she argues, 'has become focused on a number of questions concerning the role and the status of "femininity" in the conceptual frame of philosophic discourse.' ... This interest appears to be 'an extraordinary co-occurence of phenomena: the rebirth of the women's movement, on the one hand, and the need to reexamine the foundations of rational discourse felt by the majority of European philosophers,' on the other.

How do the European philosophers make use of the concept of femininity in their work?

> Braidotti then goes on to discuss the various forms that femininity assumes in the work of Deleuze, Foucault, Lyotard, and Derrida, and, concurrently, the consistent refusal by each philosopher to identify femininity with real women. On the contrary, it is only by giving up the insistence on sexual specificity (gender) that women, in their eyes, would be the social group best qualified (because they are oppressed by sexuality) to foster a radically 'other' subject, de-centered and de-sexualised. ... In other words, only by denying sexual difference (and gender) as components of subjectivity in real women, and hence by denying the history of women's political oppression and resistance, as well as the epistemological contribution of feminism to the redefinition of subjectivity and sociality, can the philosophers see in 'women' the privileged repository of 'the future of mankind.' That, Braidotti observes, 'is nothing but the old mental habit [of philosophers] of thinking the masculine as synonymous with universal ... the mental habit of translating women into metaphor' ... (pp. 23–4)

Theory, then, acts as just another agent of social control, pushing women back into the box of gender. As women seeking to climb out of the box, we are unable really to conceptualise a world where gender does not constrain us. Androgyny is not the way forward, nor is the celebration of female difference (foolish, in the light of political reality). What, then, is the possible route out? De Lauretis argues that in effect we are in a transitional moment as feminists, and that we must rely upon the bedrock of the women's movement, namely, the consciousness and the experience of women themselves. Both as gendered subjects who have been shaped and controlled by the technologies of gender, but also as agents who are attempting to create something else, in what she calls the micropolitical interstices, we need to call upon the evidence of real women experiencing this historical moment.

I find particularly useful the way de Lauretis speaks about the way gender is subjectively experienced by feminists seeking, as it were, to contest the rules.

> I had absorbed as my experience (through my own history and engagement in social reality and in the gendered spaces of feminist communities) the analytical and critical method of feminism, the *practice* of self-consciousness. For the understanding of one's personal condition as a woman in terms social and political, and the constant revision, reevaluation, and reconceptualisation of that condition in relation to other women's understanding of their sociosexual positions, generate a mode of apprehension of all social reality that derives from the consciousness of gender. (p.20)

Or, in a slightly different formulation, de Lauretis refers to

> the experience of gender, the meaning, effects and self-representations produced in the subject by the sociocultural practices, discourses, and institutions devoted to the production of men and women. (p. 19)

What she sees feminists as doing is the work of carving

> out spaces in the margins of hegemonic discourses, social spaces carved in the interstices of institutions and in the chinks and cracks of the power-knowledge apparati. And it is there that the terms of a different construction of gender can be posed — terms that do have effect and take hold at the level of subjectivity and self-representation: in the micropolitical practices of daily life and daily resistances that afford both agency and sources of power or empowering investments; and in the cultural productions of women, feminists, which inscribe that movement in and out of ideology, that crossing back and forth of the boundaries — and of the limits — of sexual difference(s). (p. 25)

I turn now to quite a different world, namely, the account of gender in the book by Aihwa Ong on Malaysian factory women. Ong's is a study of village girls being drawn into factory work in the several so-called free trade zones established by the Malaysian government under the New Economic Policy in the decade from 1970 to 1980. Her book is extremely thorough and complex, looking at the lives of these young women in their broadest economic, social, political and cultural contexts. I will not attempt to summarise her work here as I would not be doing it justice. But I want to focus upon some of the points that she makes about the uses and abuses of gender, or what we might broadly term gender manipulation.

The setting is that government financial and labour policies have created a situation in which the lowest production costs available to the companies are obtainable by hiring a female-dominated labour force. (p. 147) Thus a generation of young women is being drawn into a new urban proletariat, and the signs and symbols of this change are everywhere. The factory girls are visibly different from the other village young women. They shop for clothes in town and they have abandoned the traditional flowing dress of the Malay peasant women for 'eyecatching' outfits and western-style make-up.

This new category of women is discussed in the press with a critical eye. Ong discusses the new 'presentation of self' by the factory women as, in part, the expression of a new-found freedom. These young women have now acquired independent incomes and correspondingly are beginning to exert a new kind of autonomy.

> Almost all factory women choose their potential spouses either directly, through correspondence, or by accepting a suitor's overtures. This autonomy was directly based on their earning power ... (p. 199)

The hostility of the more traditional village women toward the new 'electric look' — a triple pun on the 'women's industrial product, their imputed personality, and the bright city lights they supposedly seek' (p. 181) — is explicit. Ong quotes one village woman as saying,

> It is not nice the way (some factory women) attempt to imitate male style. Like, they want to be rugged. For instance, men wear 'Wrangler', they want to follow suite [sic] ... some of them straight away take on the attributes of men in their clothing, they forget their sex. (p. 199)

But of course as one would expect, the life of the newly formed female urban proletariat is not all make-up and Wranglers. The working conditions are harsh and damaging. There is a rapid turnover, as the close work required in putting together the electronic components rapidly damages eyesight and workers soon start having to wear eyeglasses. The Japanese companies prefer young 'fresh' single women between sixteen and twenty-four years of age, with only primary education, from poor families living within 20 miles of the Free Trade Zone. They are expected to have strong eyes to 'withstand intensive use of microscopes employed in the writing, bonding, and mounting processes of electronics assemblywork'. Ong quotes a chief engineer at one of the three companies where she conducted her research saying that 'the highly educated person is hard to control'. (p. 154)

And control is of course a central issue in the workplace. Ong outlines the structure of authority in the factories, with particular emphasis on the structures that are used, precisely, to exert control of this new workforce. Principal among these is the skilful use and manipulation of gender power. (In fact the title of the relevant chapter is 'The Modern Corporation: Manufacturing Gender Hierarchy'.) Ong traces the way in which the corporate managers create a pyramidal structure of the work-place to create a model of authority that evokes a family, with male authority highly visible. Each male foreman is placed in charge of ten to forty female operators, who are regularly treated with some strictness. Foremen also have the authority to determine 'special rewards or micropunishments on a daily basis'. (p. 165) Ong writes that 'it was in the daily exercise of power relations between female workers and fore-men which, because emotion-laden and infused with ambivalence, was key to enforcing work discipline'. (p. 165)

Ong documents other methods used by the companies to evoke and to reinforce the culturally-learned docility of the Malaysian peasant women workers, including regular cynical meetings with parents from the villages to demonstrate [sic] how well they are treating the daughters.

Her description of how the companies manage a surveillance and encoding of Malay female sexuality in work, housing and social relation-ships outside the workplace is intended to indicate that the main engine of control over this group of workers is not so much either the politics of communalism or the Taylorist techniques and the deskilling of labour described by Braverman[18], but rather the manipulation of gender. She evokes a

> multiplicity of overlapping disciplinary techniques which produce
> biological objects, docile bodies, and sexualised subjects in transnational
> companies. In the industrialisation of the Malaysian economy, relations of
> domination and subordination based on gender, more than ethnicity,
> became consistently salient. (p. 178)

Ong documents how the industrial situation as organised by the govern-ment precludes any unionised resistance to the ever-increasing pro-ductivity demands placed upon the Malay women factory workers. But she locates an area of resistance nonetheless in the mysterious periodical outbreaks of spirit possession on the factory floor, something that has necessitated the regular hiring by the companies of traditional Malay *bomoh* (shamans) to drive out the evil spirits that prevent the women from working and that effectively disrupt the production line for hours and sometimes for days. She writes:

> I wish to discover, in the vocabulary of spirit possession, the unconscious
> beginnings of an idiom of protest against labor discipline and male control
> in the modern industrial situation. Spirit visitations to both foreign and
> local factories with sizeable numbers of young Malay female workers
> engender devil images which dramatically reveal the contradictions
> between Malay and capitalist ways of apprehending the human condition.
> I. M. Lewis has suggested that women's spirit possession episodes are
> 'thinly disguised protest ... against the dominant sex.' By 'capitalising on
> their distress,' the victims of spirit possession called public attention to
> their subordinate position and sought to alleviate it ... In the following

cases, spirit imageries reveal not only a mode of unconscious retaliation against male authority but fundamentally a sense of dislocation in human relations and a need for greater spiritual vigilance in domains reconstituted by capitalist relations of production. (p. 207)

The incidents recounted are of course subject to a variety of interpretations, presumably. But they are real enough and often result in serious disruptions to the production system of the factories.

It was the afternoon shift, at about nine o'clock. All was quiet. Suddenly, [the victim] started sobbing, laughed, and then shrieked. She flailed at the machine . . . she was violent, she fought as the foreman and technician pulled her away. Altogether, three operators were afflicted . . . The supervisor and foremen took them to the clinic and told the driver to send them home . . . (p. 220)

One of the most vivid examples of spirit possession is the case reported in the following incident.

Workers saw "things" appear when they went to the toilet. Once, when a woman entered the toilet she saw a tall figure in the midst of licking sanitary towels [*Modess* supplied in the cabinet]. It had a long tongue, and those sanitary towels . . . cannot be used anymore. (p. 220)

Ong's informants all related these events to a series of profound disruptions to the cultural order.

People say that the workplace is haunted by the *hantu* who dwells below . . . well, this used to be all jungle, it was a burial ground before the factory was built. The devil disturbs those who have weak constitution . . . [therefore] one should guard against being easily startled, or afraid . . . Other interviews elicited the same images: the erection of the FTZ on the burial grounds of aboriginal groups; disturbed earth and grave spirits swarming through the factory premises, weretigers roaming the shopfloor. (p. 220)

What then is the meaning of these episodes of spirit possession? Ong sees them as being directly related to the upheaval in the gender identity of the young women, which she describes as follows.

Their sexuality has been mapped out as an arena of contestation . . . The *hantu* symbolism . . . spoke not of an ideology of class struggle but of the right to be treated *as human beings*. Spirit attacks were indirect retaliations against coercion and demands for justice in personal terms within the industrial milieu.(p. 220)

In other words, the spirit possession episodes are a political expression of the struggle over the definition of the meaning of gender in the context of the proletarianisation of these young women's lives. There is among anthropologists some debate over whether spirit possession is being overinterpreted in this account as in others as a kind of unconscious or preconscious workers' politics.[19] But in Ong's account, her ethnographic descriptions

> attest to the deconstructions and reconstructions of gender in the shifting webs of agency and domination within the family, the labor system, Islam, and the wider society. Malay factory women were in the process of reformulating a class sexuality. Their struggles to pose new questions and to redefine the meaning of morality represented a quest for self-determination against agencies of power and capital which treat human beings like raw resources, disposable instruments, and fractured sensibilities. (p. 221)

It seems to me that what Aihwa Ong has written is an account of how gender is actually being reconstructed at a particular historical moment, with the agents of reconstruction clearly in view. These are the Japanese companies and their local representatives and the other local players — the women; their parents; their brothers, sisters and cousins; and of course the Malaysian government and those implementing its economic policies. The activity of gender reconstruction if we can call it that is clearly visible *in medias res.*

The other point, of course, is that in Ong's view the reconstruction of gender is an arena of struggle and contest with many people seeking to control the outcome, including the women themselves whose very identity is at stake in the situation.

What, then, can we conclude about the state of play of the concept of gender from the work of these three writers? I would suggest that, at the least, we have got the basis for setting some requirements for an adequate theory of gender that remains true to the tradition of feminist struggle from which the concept gains both its force and its urgency. These — at a minimum — would be as follows.

First, the concept of gender has got to include some direct relationship to the issue of power. Theories of gender are fundamentally about relations of domination and subordination and about how these are perpetuated or contested.

Second, the concept must take account of and use the subjective experience of gender. The original concept of core gender identity in the work of the sex researchers such as Robert Stoller and John Money, and as revisited in the work of Nancy Chodorow, refers to the acquisition of a sense of gender as an intrinsic and palpable part of personal identity. It cannot be seen as something that is simply applied superficially to individuals as though they were stamped one by one as they emerged from the assembly line of the agencies of socialisation. We need more evidence of how gender identity is actually experienced. De Lauretis is eloquent on this point, in my view.[20]

In particular, the issue of thinking about intersections among race, ethnicity and gender can most fruitfully be explored by giving centrality to accounts of the experiences of those who live at the intersections. In a memorable presentation to the Critical Legal Studies Conference, Kimberle Crenshaw spoke of her experience of being Black and female as one of living, as it were, on the Los Angeles freeway. She has to look 'every which way' for the traffic of racism and sexism, and this has shaped her self-concept, her academic writing and her politics.[21]

Third, the concept has got to incorporate some notion of the possibility of transformation. Gender and how it is socially constructed is, luckily, a changing and changeable process. Otherwise as feminists we would all have to throw in the towel. But the evidence is that change is both possible and is happening.

Fourth, a concept of gender must incorporate the idea that gender and its construction and reconstruction is invariably a site of struggle and contest. This, in a way, is the most important lesson from Aihwa Ong's otherwise fairly sobering observations of the process by which the Malay peasant women are being transformed into a newly constituted proletariat. While she shows us how the Japanese companies cynically manipulate the gender assumptions both of the workers themselves and of their families, she also shows us the degree to which the young women themselves struggle as best they can to define new modes of gender identities in their own interest.

Finally, we have got somehow to get beyond the obsessive polarity and pendulum swing between sameness and difference, and get used to some new ways of thinking about gender in its social, economic and political context. It is not obvious how this can be done.[22] But I believe that there are some clues within the other points I have been making about the concept of gender.

The sameness/difference dichotomy is rooted, as MacKinnon has pointed out, in a liberal bourgeois notion of a feminism that simply makes room for women in pre-existing male structures. That is, it takes a male structured and dominated world and asks the question, should women conform to male standards or remain different from them? The fluid, moveable concept of gendered experience as described by de Lauretis, and by Ong in another, less free context, suggest that the meanings of femininity at least, if not of masculinity, shift and change with a changing set of social structures. We come back again, therefore, to an agenda of fundamental social change.

One more point, and that is that, for me, the impact of feminism is connected to the insistence upon agency, subjectivity, self-determination and self-transformation, all old universalising non-trendy humanist Western concepts, I know, but none of them yet really tested and tried out with their full implications for the women of the world. Gender theory has to cope with this, in the last analysis, if it is going to remain connected to the revolutionary feminist tradition from which it springs.

Endnotes

Chapter 2

1. See Anne Summers, 1975; Roberta Sykes, 1989.

2. See Hester Eisenstein, 1982.

3. The Mary Daly event took place on 24 August 1981; see Meaghan Morris, 1988.

4. Marian Sawer, 1990, pp. xv; xvii.

5. I have seen the word in print in only one other national context, referring to the analogous Canadian experience; see Lorna Weir, 1987. For a discussion of the Australian femocrat see *inter alia* Suzanne Franzway, 1986, pp. 45–57; and Suzanne Franzway, Dianne Court, and R.W. Connell, 1989.

6. On this point, see also Anne Summers, 1988.

7. See Eva Cox, 1985; for a full account of this strategy and its progress, see Sawer, 1990.

8. For the last of these under the Labor Government, which fell on March 19, 1988, see the "Statement" by Premier Barrie Unsworth for March, 1988, covering initiatives in child care, legal measures against rape and child sexual assault, domestic violence, women's employment and training, EEO, women in small business, housing, health, women in prison, and several other areas, including special measures for Aboriginal women; *Statement by Hon. Barrie Unsworth, MP, Premier of New South Wales and Minister Responsible for Women's Interests to International Women's Day Reception*, Sydney: NSW Government Printer, 1988. The strategy of developing a special women's budget was originally developed by Anne Summers in the Office of the Status of Women; see Marian Sawer, 1990, pp. 228–241.

9. See 'Women, The State and Your Complexion' (page 30) for more details on this debate. See also Sara Dowse, 1983a, pp. 201–21; and 1983b, pp. 139–60; Suzanne Franzway, 1986 and Suzanne Franzway et al., 1989; Sawer, 1990; and Yeatman, 1990.

10. After first developing this image, I was moved to find that Julia Ryan had come to it independently, in her account of the UN Nairobi conference in 1985: '(W)hen I asked various Forum participants how they would encapsulate Nairobi they fell into vagueness. Finally, on the last lunch of the safari, at the desert town of Narok, one of the Australian women suddenly suggested that it resembled the gnu migration, a great unstoppable movement, wandering and uncertain in some sections, determined and fastmoving in others. I had been thinking of a river entering a flood plain but the wildebeest were a more satisfactory image.' Julia Ryan, 1985.

11. At the time of writing, the world of higher education in Australia is being transformed by the sweeping changes being implemented by the Federal Minister for Employment Education, and Training, John Dawkins, which include amalgamations of colleges of advanced education with universities, and much tighter central control of funding for academic research. For a searing critique of the direction now being followed, see Hugh Stretton, 1989, pp. 30–32. It remains to be seen what impact the rush to so-called economic rationalisation will have on the fledgling development of Women's Studies programmes in Australia.

12. At this writing, Victoria, South Australia, Western Australia and (*mirabile dictu!*) Queensland. As the result of elections held in 1989, Queensland elected its first Labor government in 32 years. In Tasmania, Labor governs in coalition with the Greens (environmentalists).

13. *Refractory Girl* is the oldest feminist journal in Australia. Published in Sydney, the title alludes to the intractable nature attributed to the convict women who were shipped to Botany Bay during the period when Australia served as a penal colony for Great Britain, from 1788 to 1868. See Robert Hughes, 1987, pp. 244 ff. Australian feminists have appropriated the previously very male concept of 'mate' to mean, approximately, sister *cum* comrade.

Chapter 3

1. See Leonie Kramer, 1985.

2. See Hester Eisenstein, 1985c.

3. Jozefa Sobski, 1985.

4. See Ann Game, 1984, pp. 253–57, and Gretchen Poiner and Sue Wills, 1991.

5. Like that by Eva Cox. See Eva Cox, 1985.

6. Instead of its correct title, the Office for the Status of Women. Ironically this epithet had its origins among the femocrats on the staff of the Women's Bureau in the then Department of Employment and Industrial Relations, who were critical of the OSW for what they saw as its lack of attention to working class women's issues. See Marian Sawer, 1990, p. 76.

7. See Eva Cox, 1985, p. 14.

8. For an alternative definition of mandarins in this context, see Anne Summers, 1986, pp. 59–67. Her point in this article is that to the women's movement, femocrats appear to be mandarins, like their male peers in the public service. But to the real mandarins, as it were, the femocrats are outsiders, interlopers, whose commitment to the values of the permanent public service is always suspect by definition.

9. See for example Lesley Lynch, 1984, pp. 38–44.

10. Although they are often from a background that makes them familiar with the issues of impoverished women. In interviews with present and former femocrats for a forthcoming study, I found many instances of women who were the first in their families to attend university.

11. RSI is the Australian term for what is called "carpal tunnel syndrome" in the United States. This is a condition of strain from repetitive work at keyboards, or in factory processing work, now gaining widespread attention in the United States, particularly in the chicken preparation industry. The condition is widespread in areas of traditionally women's work and in terminal stages is severely crippling. For an account of Australian female trade union leadership, see Anna Booth and Linda Rubenstein, 1990, pp. 121–135.

12. See the classic article by Jo Freeman ('Joreen'), 1973, pp. 285–99.

13. Ann Snitow, 1985, p. 53.

14. Quoted in Suzanne Gordon, 1985, p. 43.

15. Miriam Dixson, 1986, pp. 23–4.

16. Francoise Ducrocq, 1985, p. 65.

Chapter 4

1. Catharine A. MacKinnon, 1983, p. 682. MacKinnon has since sought to remedy this omission (see MacKinnon, 1989). I persist with this inquiry despite the provocative and interesting argument set forth by Judith Allen in Allen, 1990, pp. 21–35. See p. 34, where Allen concludes that a theory of the state is 'not an

GENDER SHOCK

indigenous feminist need', but a category of analysis imported from Marxism and liberalism.

2. See Suzanne Franzway, 1986, for a sceptical interpretation of the femocracy.

3. Papers from the conference were collected in a supplementary issue of *Signs* (5, 3, Spring, 1980), and then as a book: see Catharine R. Stimpson, 1981.

4. See Nancy C.M. Hartsock, 1983.

5. For a further discussion of this concept, in the context of the feminist critique of science, see Sandra Harding, 1986.

6. See Mary Fainsod Katzenstein and Carol M. Mueller, 1987, for one account.

7. See Lynne Segal, 1987.

8. MacKinnon has also been a leader in establishing sexual harassment as a harm under the law, for which women can collect damages. See Lucinda Finley, 1988, p. 353: '[MacKinnon's] work has been profoundly important, because in naming women's experiences and injuries — as, for example, in her book *Sexual Harassment of Working Women [: A Case of Sex Discrimination, 1979]* — she has forced the legal system to recognize these injuries as systematic products of male domination and as instances of discrimination'. On the legislation and its fate, see Catharine A. MacKinnon, 1987, pp. 163ff.; in this volume MacKinnon presents a more nuanced account of the role of law.

9. Gillian Calvert, 1987, p. 2.

10. *ibid.*

11. See Lesley Lynch, 1984. The femocrat cartoon is reproduced in Marian Sawer, 1990, p. 26.

12. Several volumes have now appeared that begin to undertake this task. See Sophie Watson, 1990; Suzanne Franzway et al., 1989; Marian Sawer, 1990; and Anna Yeatman, 1990.

13. This point was made to me by Suzanne Franzway, in a discussion prior to the presentation of our papers on 14 July 1987 at the SAANZ conference. Note that all comments in this chapter refer to New South Wales prior to the election of the Liberal–National coalition government on 19 March 1988.

14. For an example of such an analysis, see Ann Game, 1984.

15. This is the kind of framework sketched out in Suzanne Franzway et al., 1989.

16. Remark by Margaret Vickers, at the Public Policy Program seminar convened by Professor Jane Marceau at the Australian National University, October 1984. This exchange took place during an official seminar series convened by the Public Service Board in Canberra, at which Vickers — the most senior woman there, but junior relative to the other very senior officers present — was chairing the session. (Conversation with Margaret Vickers, Berkshire Conference of Women Historians, Rutgers University, June, 1990). Her choice of agencies is not casual, given the point about exclusion of femocrats from the mainstream.

17. See Zillah Eisenstein, 1981, *passim.*

18. A good starting point is the thoughtful piece of work by Rosie Wagstaff, 1986.

19. See Chris Ronalds, 1987; Peter Wilenski, 1977; Peter Wilenski, 1982; and Alison Ziller, 1980.

20. On this topic, see Lois Bryson, 1987, pp. 259–73, and Michael Pusey, 1988, pp. 21–26. On economic rationalism in the Commonwealth public service, see Michael Pusey, 1991.

21. For the documentation of these changes, see the Annual Reports from the Director of Equal Opportunity in Public Employment, which appear as chapters in Anti-Discrimination Board of New South Wales, 1981–1988.

22. Debate over comparable worth strategy, Women's Electoral Lobby National Agenda Conference, Canberra, April, 1986; for Edna Ryan's analysis, see Edna Ryan, 1988, pp. 7–16.

23. See Clare Burton, 1987, pp. 424–35.

24. See Suzanne Franzway, 1986.

Chapter 5

1. See for example Sophie Watson, 1990; and Mary Fainsod Katzenstein and Carol M. Mueller eds, 1987.

2. The example of trade unions is not directly relevant to the material presented here, but is one of the fundamental differences that I believe has shaped the femocratic phenomenon, in that the traditional underlying assumptions about worker entitlements in Australia are part of a political climate that has made room, over time, for some feminist claims — although not without long and hard struggles! On what follows, see Edna Ryan, 1988 and Clare Burton et al., 1987.

3. I enter a caveat here, as my data base is idiosyncratic. Clare Burton has suggested to me that I am perhaps comparing apples to oranges, and that rather than comparing Australia to the United States, I am in fact contrasting the international culture of Women's Studies to the international culture of feminist activism in government and union circles. Burton is an expert on comparable worth and equal employment opportunity in Australia, who was appointed Director of Equal Opportunity in Public Employment by the Liberal–National government of New South Wales in 1988.

4. For a preliminary account of Australian feminist interventions see Sophie Watson, 1990. For an account of the special treatment/equal treatment debate in law see Lucinda M. Finley, 1986, pp. 1118–1182. On the legislation defining pornography as a civil rights violation, see Catharine A. MacKinnon, 1987, pp. 163–197.

5. For more details on the operations of the legislation, see Hester Eisenstein, 1985a, pp. 72–83. On the Australian context of affirmative action legislation, see Marian Sawer, 1985, *passim*, and Chris Ronalds, 1987. The ambiguity of the traditional categories for affirmative action target groups was never really clarified under the New South Wales legislation, namely, the overlapping of categories (Aboriginal women; women with physical disabilities). The EEO programme was thus always vulnerable to the not unfair criticism that when 'women' were discussed, this meant, in effect, white women.

6. Ironically during these years the American tradition of affirmative action and anti-discrimination legislation was being eroded by a series of Supreme Court decisions. For a summary of these events see Alan Freeman, 'Anti-Discrimination Law: The View from 1989', in David Kairys, ed., *The Politics of Law*, 2nd edn, New York: Pantheon, 1990. The proposed Civil Rights Act of 1990 was intended to undo some of the damage.

7. Peter Wilenski, 1977; Alison Ziller, 1980.

8. The New South Wales state administration comprised two kinds of bodies: departments, operating under a single piece of public service legislation, the Public Service Act of 1979; and the declared authorities, each operating under its own enabling legislation. I elaborate on this point below.

9. Thus the Department of Education operated under the Education Commission Act of 1980.

10. Since the reforms undertaken in response to the Scott review under the Greiner Liberal–National government in 1989 and 1990, this description is no longer accurate. One of the aims of this reform has been to decentralise power in the Department. There have been significant cuts, as well, to the teaching force.

11. This was the concept of representative bureaucracy, introduced into the discourse of the New South Wales state administration by Peter Wilenski; see Peter Wilenski, 1977.

12. See Anti-Discrimination Board, 1981–1988.

13. The politics of the Teachers Federation in relation to the package, under the leadership of its first woman president, Jennie George, makes an extremely interesting sub-plot, which I am omitting for reasons of space and lack of direct information.

14. From the Department of Education, 1985.

15. I may be overstating the case for Labor here; Marian Sawer emphasises the impact of feminist interventions within the Liberal–National coalition parties as well as within the Labor party, especially under the Fraser government; see Marian Sawyer, 1990, pp. 33ff.

16. See Adrienne Rich, 1976, chapter 9, 'Motherhood and Daughterhood'.

17. In this context it is interesting to note the arrival of a crop of publications treating of competition among women. See for example Louise Eichenbaum and Susie Orbach, 1988; and Valerie Miner and Helen E. Longino eds., 1987.

18. See Anna Yeatman, 1988.

19. See Scott Heller, 1988, pp. 1, A6.

20. For a study that begins to address this problem by bringing together and comparing a range of feminist political and academic perspectives, see M.E. Hawkesworth, 1990.

Chapter 6

1. See Hester Eisenstein and Alice Jardine, 1980.

2. Hester Eisenstein, 1984, and Alice Jardine, 1985.

3. See for example, Linda J. Nicholson, 1990; Chris Weedon, 1987; Meaghan Morris, 1988; and Elizabeth Grosz, 1989.

4. *Copyright* 1, 1 (1987): 'Fin-de-Siècle 2000'.

Chapter 7

1. It was subsequently published in *Taking Issue: Grace Vaughan Memorial*

Lecture and Octagon Lectures, 1986, Perth: University of Western Australia Extension, 1987.

2. See Nancy Hartsock, 1983.

3. See R. W. Connell, 1986b, pp. 342–3.

4. See Patricia Giles, 1985, pp. 111 ff., and Julia Ryan, 1985, pp. 116 ff.

5. Anne Summers, 1986, p. 59. With the advent of Labor Governments in Tasmania and Queensland, the establishment of women's advisory units and equal employment opportunity boards is now under way in those states as well.

6. ibid, p. 65.

7. See Dorothy Wickenden, 1986, p. 20. For April, 1990 the figure is 1272; 'Women in Elective Office, 1989' (fact sheet, amended, April 1990), Center for the American Woman and Politics, National Information Bank on Women in Public Office, Eagleton Institute of Politics, Rutgers University.

8. See 'Women to the Fore in Norwegian Government', *Sydney Morning Herald,* 16 May 1986.

9. Dorothy Wickenden, 1986, p. 21.

10. On some of the complexities of the relationships among women in bureaucratic hierarchies, and especially between feminists and clerical workers, see Rosemary Pringle, 1988.

11. Marilyn Lake, 1986, p. 146.

12. See Hester Eisenstein, 1984.

13. Pete Hamill, 1986, p. 11.

14. This is still the policy toward women in the United States armed forces. See Elaine Sciolino, 1990, p. D 23: women 'fill a variety of dangerous, theoretically non-combat roles, from aerial refueling in the 1986 Libya raid to making up 25 percent of the 1,000 crew members on the repair ship Arcadia, which steamed into the Persian Gulf after an Iraqi plane struck the frigate Stark'.

15. Marilyn Lake, 1986, p. 135.

16. For further discussion of the media coverage of the Greenham women, see Julia Emberley and Donna Landry, 1989, pp. 485–498.

17. Sara Ruddick, 1980, pp. 342–67.

18. Carol Johnson, 1985, p. 148.

19. See R.W. Connell, 1986a, p. 36, and Joyce Stevens, 1986, p. 154.

20. Patrick Thorne, 1986, p. 4.

21. Sara Ruddick, 1980, p. 351. A revised statement of this idea appears in Ruddick, 1989, pp. 74–75. See this volume, *passim*, for the full development of Ruddick's concept of maternal thinking.

22. See Sheila Rowbotham, 1985, pp. 49–63.

23. Sara Ruddick, 1980, p. 361.

24. Sheila Rowbotham, 1985, p. 52.

Chapter 8

1. See Jane Flax, 1983, pp. 21–40.

2. See Lisa Duggan, 1986, pp. 13–14.

3. Paraphrased in Zillah Eisenstein, 1983, p. 56.

4. See Barbara Ehrenreich, 1983, *passim*; Michèle Barrett and Mary McIntosh, 1982, pp. 13 ff.

5. See Juliet Mitchell, 1971; Rayna Rapp, Ellen Ross and Renate Bridenthal, 1979, pp. 174–200.

6. See Jane Flax, 1983, pp. 21 ff.

7. See Gayle Rubin, 1975, pp. 157–210.

8. See Nancy Chodorow, 1978; Adrienne Rich, 1976; and Sara Ruddick, 1989.

9. On this tradition of social theory, see Jessica Benjamin, 1988, p. 246, n. 4 and *passim*.

10. See Dorothy Dinnerstein, 1977; and Jane Flax, 1980, pp. 20–40.

11. In this very rapid overview I am not venturing into the quite different set of formulations of these problems derived from Lacanian analysis and certain

strands of French feminist theory. On this see Toril Moi, 1985, *inter alia*.

12. Monique Wittig, 1971; Charlotte Perkins Gilman, 1979. For a study covering these plus some more modern utopian feminist fiction, see Frances Bartkowski, 1989.

13. See Mary Daly, 1978.

14. See Hester Eisenstein, 1984, especially chapter 13. For the context of the development of radical feminist ideas, see Alice Echols, 1989.

15. See R. D. Laing, 1971, *inter alia*.

16. See Meredith Edwards, 1985, pp. 95–103.

17. See Judith Allen, 1986. Lindy Chamberlain has now been exonerated of the charge of murdering her baby. But Allen raises the point of the symbolic weight of the murder charge, given the deep familiarity of most mothers with feelings of murderous rage toward their infant children.

18. On this point, cf. Renate Bridenthal, 1982, p. 234.

19. See Eva Cox, 1987.

20. Linda Gordon, 1982, p. 51.

Chapter 9

1. See Elizabeth Spelman, 1988. I have recklessly oversimplified here what is a complex and thoughtful argument about the terms 'woman' and 'gender' in relation to race, ethnicity, and questions of essentialism, among other issues.

2. See Denise Thompson, 1989, pp. 23–32. See also Anne Edwards, 1989, pp. 1–12; Genevieve Lloyd, 1989, pp. 13–22; and Moira Gatens, 1989, pp. 33–47.

3. Cf. for example the joyous language used in the address by Caryn McTigh Musil, National Director, at the opening session of the Eleventh Annual Conference of the National Women's Studies Association, Towson State University, Towson, Maryland, 14–18 June 1989, and in the conference theme, 'Feminist Transformations'.

4. For a guide to these developments see *inter alia* Ellen Carol Dubois, Gail Paradise Kelly, Elizabeth Lapovsky Kennedy, Carolyn W. Korsmeyer and Lillian S. Robinson, 1987.

5. On what follows, see Hester Eisenstein, 1984, and Hester Eisenstein and Alice Jardine, 1980.

6. On the dangers of curtailing discussion by use of 'essentialism' as a feminist term of abuse, see Nancy K. Miller, 1988, pp. 116; 240; and *passim*.

7. On the question of whether or not the work of poststructuralists and deconstructionists represents a genuine possibility of alliance with feminism, I refer the reader to the complex and savvy writing of Alice Jardine in *Gynesis*; and see 'Harvard and New South Wales'. See also the issue of *Feminist Studies* on deconstruction, 14 (1988), especially Joan W. Scott, 'Deconstructing Equality-Versus-Difference: Or, the Uses of Poststructuralist Theory for Feminism', pp. 33–50.

8. See Carol Gilligan, 1982.

9. For a thorough historical and contemporary review of this set of issues, see Carol Bacchi, 1990.

10. In feminist jurisprudence this conflict is referred to as 'equal treatment' vs. 'special treatment'. On the issue of maternity benefits, see Lucinda Finley, 1986, pp. 1118–82; see also the discussion in Frances Olsen, 1986, pp. 1518–41, which places this debate in the historical context of the debate over protective labour legislation for women. I am grateful to Regina Graycar, of the University of New South Wales Law School, for introducing me to this literature.

11. For a review of the comparable worth campaign in the United States, see Sara M. Evans and Barbara J. Nelson, 1989.

12. Nancy F. Cott, 1987, convincingly illustrates the fact that the sameness/difference schism within feminism dates at least from the winning of the vote in the United States in 1920, and has its roots in the writings of the first self-proclaimed feminists of the 1910s. It is an open question whether this is to be considered comforting or discouraging to contemporary feminists.

13. See for example Michèle Barrett, 1988.

14. R.W. Connell, 1987, p. x.

15. In discussion at the Feminism and Legal Theory Conference: Women and Power, University of Wisconsin–Madison, 27 June–2 July, 1988; on de Lauretis, see below.

16. Catharine MacKinnon, 1982; and 1983, pp. 635–58. See also Catharine MacKinnon, 1989.

17. R. W. Connell, 1987.

18. See Harry Braverman, 1974.

19. Comments by Joel Kahn, Professor of Anthropology, Department of Anthropology and Sociology, Monash University, August 1988.

20. See Nancy Chodorow, 1978. I am aware that in this formulation I am leaving the status of individual gender experience 'unproblematised' in the poststructuralist sense. At this writing I am not yet convinced that this is such a bad thing to do.

21. Plenary Session, 'Women of Color and Feminism', 11th National Conference on Critical Legal Studies, 2 October 1988, American University, Washington D.C.

22. Joan Scott argues that poststructuralism offers some indications of a way out of the sameness/difference impasse; see Joan Scott, 1988.

Bibliography

Allen, Judith (1986) discussion of Azaria Chamberlain case, *The Coming Out Show* ABC Radio (Sydney), October, 1986.

Allen, Judith (1990) 'Does Feminism Need A Theory of "the State"?,' in Sophie Watson ed. *Playing the State: Australian Feminist Interventions* Sydney: Allen & Unwin.

Anti-Discrimination Board of New South Wales (1981–1988) *Annual Report* Sydney: New South Wales Government Printer.

Bacchi, Carol (1990) *Same Difference: Feminism and Sexual Difference* Sydney: Allen & Unwin.

Baldock, Cora and Cass, Bettina, eds (1983) *Women, Social Welfare and the State,* Sydney: Allen & Unwin.

Barrett, Michèle (1988) *Women's Oppression Today: The Marxist-Feminist Encounter* London: Verso.

Barrett, Michèle, and McIntosh, Mary (1982) *The Anti-Social Family,* London: Verso/NLB.

Bartkowski, Frances (1989) *Feminist Utopias* Lincoln: University of Nebraska Press.

Benjamin, Jessica (1988) *The Bonds of Love: Psychoanalysis, Feminism, and the Problem of Domination* New York: Pantheon.

Booth, Anna and Rubenstein, Linda (1990) 'Women in Trade Unions in Australia' in Sophie Watson ed. *Playing the State: Australian Feminist Interventions* Sydney: Allen & Unwin.

Braverman, Harry (1974) *Labor and Monopoly Capital* New York: Monthly Review Press.

Bridenthal, Renate (1982) 'The Family: The View from a Room of Her Own' in Barrie Thorne and Marilyn Yalom, eds *Rethinking the Family: Some Feminist Questions* New York: Longman.

Brennan, Deborah and O'Donnell, Carol (1986) *Caring for Australia's Children: Political and Industrial Issues in Child Care* Sydney: Allen & Unwin.

Broom, Dorothy ed. (1983) *Unfinished Business: Social Justice for Women in Australia* Sydney: Allen & Unwin.

Bryson, Lois (1987) 'Women and Management in the Public Sector' *Australian Journal of Public Administration* 46.

Burton, Clare (1987) 'Merit and Gender: Organisations and the "Mobilisation of Masculine Bias"' *Australian Journal of Social Issues* 22.

Burton, Clare et al. (1987) *Women's Worth: Pay Equity and Job Evaluation in Australia* Canberra: Australian Government Printing Service.

Calvert, Gillian (1987) 'Feminism in the Public Service' *Hersay: News Bulletin from the New South Wales Women's Advisory Council* 4.

Campbell, Beatrix (1983) lecture, New South Wales Teachers Federation House, Sydney, 13 April.

Chodorow, Nancy (1978) *The Reproduction of Mothering: Psychoanalysis and the Sociology of Gender* Berkeley: University of California Press.

Connell, R.W. (1986a) 'Socialism: Moving On' in David McKnight ed. *Moving Left: The Future of Socialism in Australia* Sydney and London: Pluto Press.

Connell, R.W. (1986b) 'Theorising Gender' in Norma Grieve and Ailsa Burns, eds *Australian Women: New Feminist Perspectives* Melbourne: Oxford University Press.

Connell, R. W. (1987) *Gender and Power: Society, The Person and Sexual Politics*, Stanford: Stanford University Press.

Copyright (1987) 1, 1 : 'Fin-de-Siècle 2000'.

Cott, Nancy F. (1987) *The Grounding of Modern Feminism* New Haven: Yale University Press.

Cox, Eva (1985) 'A Decade for Women, or The Decayed Women's Issues' *Labor Forum* 7, 2 June; reprinted in *WEL-Informed: Monthly Newsletter of the NSW Women's Electoral Lobby* 149, September 1985.

Cox, Eva (1987) 'Child Abuse: Epidemic or Folk Panic? Practising Inadequate Theory' in *Refractory Girl* 30 (Sept).

Crenshaw, Kimberle (1988) address, Plenary Session, 'Women of Color and Feminism', 11th National Conference on Critical Legal Studies, 2 October, American University, Washington D.C.

Daly, Mary (1978) *Gyn/Ecology: The Metaethics of Radical Feminism* Boston: Beacon.

Daly, Mary (1984), *Pure Lust: Elemental Feminist Philosophy* Boston: Beacon.

de Lauretis, Teresa ed. (1986) *Feminist Studies/Critical Studies* Bloomington: Indiana University Press.

de Lauretis, Teresa (1987) 'The Technology of Gender' in *Technologies of Gender: Essays on Theory, Film, and Fiction* Bloomington: Indiana University Press.

Department of Education (1985) *EEO Management Plan for the Education Teaching Service* Sydney: New South Wales Government Printer.

Diamond, Irene ed. (1983) *Families, Politics and Public Policy: A Feminist Dialogue on Women and the State* New York: Longman.

Dinnerstein, Dorothy (1977) *The Mermaid and the Minotaur: Sexual Arrangements and Human Malaise* New York: Harper and Row.

Dixson, Miriam (1986) 'Gender, Class, and the Women's Movements In Australia, 1880, 1980' in Norma Grieve and Ailsa Burns, eds *Australian Women: New Feminist Perspectives* Melbourne: Oxford University Press.

Dowse, Sara (1983a) 'The Women's Movement Fandango with the State: Some Thoughts on the Movement's Role in Public Policy Since 1972' in Cora Baldock and Bettina Cass, eds *Women, Social Welfare and the State* Sydney: Allen & Unwin.

Dowse, Sara (1983b) 'The Bureaucrat as Usurer' in Dorothy Broom, ed.

Unfinished Business: Social Justice for Women in Australia Sydney: Allen & Unwin.

Dubois, Ellen Carol, Kelly, Gail Paradise, Kennedy, Elizabeth Lapovsky, Korsmeyer, Carolyn W. and Robinson, Lillian S. (1987) *Feminist Scholarship: Kindling in the Groves of Academe* Urbana and Chicago: University of Illinois Press.

Ducrocq, Francoise (1985) 'The Women's Liberation Movement in Socialist France: Four Years Later' *M/F* 10.

Duggan, Lisa (1986) 'History Between the Sheets: Politics Go Under Cover' *Village Voice Literary Supplement*, September.

Echols, Alice (1989) *Daring to Be Bad: Radical Feminism in America, 1967-1975* Minneapolis: University of Minnesota Press.

Edwards, Anne (1989) 'The Sex/Gender Distinction: Has It Outlived Its Usefulness?' *Australian Feminist Studies* 10 (Summer).

Edwards, Meredith (1985) 'Individual Equity and Social Policy' in Carole Pateman and Jacqueline Goodnow, eds *Women, Social Science and Public Policy* Sydney: Allen & Unwin.

Ehrenreich, Barbara (1983) *The Hearts of Men: American Dreams and the Flight from Commitment* London: Pluto Press.

Eichenbaum, Louise and Orbach, Susie (1988) *Between Women: Love, Envy and Competition in Women's Friendships* New York: Viking.

Eisenstein, Hester (1982) review Laura Lederer ed. *Take Back the Night* in *Refractory Girl* 23 (March).

Eisenstein, Hester (1984) *Contemporary Feminist Thought* London and Sydney: Allen & Unwin.

Eisenstein, Hester (1985a) 'Affirmative Action at Work in New South Wales' in Marian Sawer, ed. *Program for Change: Affirmative Action in Australia* Sydney: Allen & Unwin.

Eisenstein, Hester (1985b) 'The Gender of Bureaucracy: Reflections on Feminism and the State' in Carole Pateman and Jacqueline Goodnow, eds *Women, Social Science and Public Policy* Sydney: Allen & Unwin.

Eisenstein, Hester (1985c) paper presented to FAUSA National Conference, 'Women in Post-Secondary Education: Issues and Strategies, 1975-1995', New South Wales Institute of Technology, 29-31 March, *Refractory Girl* 28 (May).

Eisenstein, Hester and Jardine, Alice eds (1980) *The Future of Difference*, Boston: G.K. Hall & Co.; reprinted, New Brunswick: Rutgers University Press, 1985.

Eisenstein, Zillah R. (1981) *The Radical Future of Liberal Feminism*, New York: Longman.

Eisenstein, Zillah R. (1983) 'The State, the Patriarchal Family, and Working Mothers,' in Irene Diamond ed. *Families, Politics and Public Policy: A Feminist Dialogue on Women and the State* New York: Longman.

Eisenstein, Zillah R. (1988) *The Female Body and the Law* Berkeley: University of California Press.

Emberley, Julia and Landry, Donna (1989) 'Coverage of Greenham and Greenham as "Coverage"' *Feminist Studies* 15, 3 (Fall).

Evans, Sara M. and Nelson, Barbara J. (1989) *Wage Justice: Comparable Worth and the Paradox of Technocratic Reform* Chicago: University of Chicago Press.

Ferguson, Kathy E. (1984) *The Feminist Case Against Bureaucracy*, Philadelphia: Temple University Press.

Finley, Lucinda M. (1986) 'Transcending Equality Theory: A Way Out of the Maternity and the Workplace Debate' *Columbia Law Review* 86.

Finley, Lucinda M. (1988) 'Review Essay – The Nature of Domination and the Nature of Women: Reflections on Feminism Unmodified' *Northwestern University Law Review* 82, 2.

Flax, Jane (1980) 'Mother-Daughter Relationships: Psychodynamics, Politics, and Philosophy' in Hester Eisenstein and Alice Jardine, eds *The Future of Difference* Boston: G.K. Hall & Co.

Flax, Jane (1983) 'Contemporary American Families: Decline or Transformation?' in Irene Diamond, eds *Families, Politics and Public Policy: A Feminist Dialogue on Women and the State* New York: Longman.

Franzway, Suzanne (1986) 'With Problems of Their Own: Femocrats and the Welfare State' *Australian Feminist Studies* 3 (Summer).

Franzway, Suzanne, Court, Dianne and Connell, R.W. (1989) *Staking a Claim: Feminism, Bureaucracy and the State* Boston: Unwin Hyman.

Freeman, Alan (1990) 'Anti-Discrimination Law: The View from 1989' in David Kairys ed. *The Politics of Law* 2nd edn, New York: Pantheon.

Freeman, Jo ('Joreen') (1973) 'The Tyranny of Structurelessness' in A. Koedt et al. *Radical Feminism* New York: Quadrangle (New York Times Book Co.).

Game, Ann (1984) 'Affirmative Action: Liberal Rationality or Challenge to Patriarchy?' *Legal Service Bulletin* 19, 6 (December).

Gatens, Moira (1989) 'Woman and Her Double(s): Sex, Gender and Ethics' *Australian Feminist Studies* 10 (Summer).

Gelb, Joyce and Palley, Marion Lier (1986) *Women and Public Policies* rev. ed. Princeton: Princeton University Press.

Giles, Patricia (1985) 'Nairobi Conference: The End of a Decade' *Australian Feminist Studies* 1 (Summer).

Gilligan, Carol (1982) *In a Different Voice* Cambridge: Harvard University Press.

Gilman, Charlotte Perkins (1979) *Herland* ed. Ann J. Lane, New York: Pantheon.

Gordon, Linda (1982) 'Why Nineteenth-Century Feminists Did Not Support "Birth Control" and Twentieth-Century Feminists Do: Feminism, Reproduction, and the Family' in Barrie Thorne and Marilyn Yalom, eds *Rethinking the Family: Some Feminist Questions* New York: Longman.

Gordon, Suzanne (1985) 'Anger, Power, and Women's Sense of Self: New Thoughts on a Psychology for the Future from Jean Baker Miller' *Ms.* July.

Grieve, Norma, and Burns, Ailsa eds (1986) *Australian Women: New Feminist Perspectives* Melbourne: Oxford University Press.

Grosz, Elizabeth (1989) *Sexual Subversions: Three French Feminists* Sydney: Allen & Unwin.

Hamill, Pete (1986) 'At Throttle Up' *Village Voice*, 11 February.

Harding, Sandra (1986) *The Science Question in Feminism* Ithaca: Cornell University Press.

Hartsock, Nancy C.M. (1983) *Money, Sex and Power: Toward a Feminist Historical Materialism* New York and London: Longman.

Hawkesworth, M.E. (1990) *Beyond Oppression: Feminist Theory and Political Strategy* New York: Continuum.

Heller, Scott (1988) 'Scholars Grapple With Literary Critic's Early Writings for

Pro-Nazi Periodical' *The Chronicle of Higher Education* 11 May.

Hughes, Robert (1987) *The Fatal Shore* New York: Alfred A. Knopf.

Jardine, Alice (1985) *Gynesis: Configurations of Woman and Modernity* Ithaca: Cornell University Press.

Johnson, Carol (1985) review essay, Marian Sawer and Marian Simms, *A Woman's Place* in *Australian Feminist Studies*, 1 (Summer).

Kairys, David ed. (1990) *The Politics of Law*, 2nd ed. New York: Pantheon.

Katzenstein, Mary Fainsod and Mueller, Carol M. eds. (1987) *The Women's Movements in the United States and Western Europe* Philadelphia: Temple University Press.

Kramer, Leonie (1985) 'Feminism's Fantasies and Fallacies' *Sydney Morning Herald* 28 March; reprinted *Refractory Girl* 28 (May).

Laing, R.D. (1971) *The Politics of the Family and Other Essays* New York: Pantheon.

Lake, Marilyn (1986) 'A Question of Time' in David McKnight ed. *Moving Left: The Future of Socialism in Australia* Sydney and London: Pluto Press.

Lloyd, Genevieve (1989) 'Woman as Other: Sex, Gender, and Subjectivity' *Australian Feminist Studies* 10 (Summer).

Lynch, Lesley (1984) 'Bureaucratic Feminisms: Bossism and Beige Suits' *Refractory Girl* 27 (May).

MacKinnon, Catharine A. (1982) 'Feminism, Marxism, Method and the State: An Agenda for Theory' *Signs*, 7, 3 (Spring).

MacKinnon, Catharine A. (1983) 'Feminism, Marxism, Method and the State: Toward a Feminist Jurisprudence' *Signs*, 8, 4 (Summer).

MacKinnon, Catharine A. (1987) 'Francis Biddle's Sister: Pornography, Civil Rights, and Speech' in *Feminism Unmodified: Discourses on Life and Law* Cambridge: Harvard University Press.

MacKinnon, Catharine A. (1987) *Feminism Unmodified: Discourses on Life and Law* Cambridge: Harvard University Press.

MacKinnon, Catharine A. (1989) *Toward a Feminist Theory of the State* Cambridge: Harvard University Press.

McKnight, David ed. (1986) *Moving Left: The Future of Socialism in Australia*, Sydney and London: Pluto Press.

Miles, Angela (1985) *Feminist Radicalism in the 1980's* Montreal: Culture Texts.

Miles, Angela and Finn, Geraldine eds. (1989) *Feminism: From Pressure to Politics* Montreal: Black Rose Books.

Miller, Nancy K. (1988) *Subject to Change: Reading Feminist Writing*, New York: Columbia University Press.

Miner, Valerie and Longino, Helen E. eds (1987) *Competition: A Feminist Taboo?* New York: The Feminist Press.

Mitchell, Juliet (1971) *Woman's Estate* New York: Vintage.

Moi, Toril (1985) *Sexual/Textual Politics: Feminist Literary Theory* London: Methuen.

Morris, Meaghan (1988) 'A-Mazing Grace: Notes on Mary Daly's Poetics' *The Pirate's Fiancée: Feminism, Reading, Postmodernism* London: Verso.

Morris, Meaghan (1988) *The Pirate's Fiancée: Feminism, Reading, Postmodernism* London: Verso.

Musil, Caryn McTigh (1989) address to the opening session of the Eleventh

Annual Conference of the National Women's Studies Association, Towson State University, Towson, Maryland, 14–18 June.

Nicholson, Linda J. ed. (1990) *Feminism/Postmodernism* New York: Routledge.

O'Donnell, Carol and Hall, Philippa (1988) *Getting Equal: Labor Market Regulation and Women's Work* Sydney: Allen & Unwin.

Olsen, Frances (1986) 'From False Paternalism to False Equality: Assaults on Feminist Community, Illinois 1869–1895' *Michigan Law Review* 84.

Ong, Aihwa (1987) *Spirits of Resistance and Capitalist Discipline: Factory Women in Malaysia* Albany: SUNY Press at Albany.

Pateman, Carole and Goodnow, Jacqueline eds (1985) *Women, Social Science and Public Policy* Sydney: Allen & Unwin.

Pateman, Carole and Grosz, Elizabeth eds (1986) *Feminist Challenges: Social and Political Theory* Sydney: Allen & Unwin.

Poiner, Gretchen and Wills, Sue (1991) *The Gifthorse* Sydney: Allen & Unwin.

Pringle, Rosemary (1988) *Secretaries Talk: Sexuality, Power, and Work* Sydney: Allen & Unwin.

Pusey, Michael (1988) 'From Canberra the Outlook is Dry' *Australian Society* July.

Pusey, Michael (1991) *Economic Rationalism in Canberra: A Nation-Building State Changes Its Mind* London, New York, Sydney: Cambridge University Press, forthcoming.

[Rapp] Reiter, Rayna ed. (1975) *Toward an Anthropology of Women* New York: Monthly Review Press.

Rapp, Rayna (1986) 'Is the Legacy of Second Wave Feminism Post-feminism?' *Socialist Review* 88, 1 (January-March).

Rapp, Rayna, Ross, Ellen and Bridenthal, Renate (1979) 'Examining Family History' *Feminist Studies* 5, 1.

Rich, Adrienne (1976) *Of Woman Born: Motherhood as Experience and Institution* New York: W. W. Norton.

Ronalds, Chris (1987) *Affirmative Action and Sex Discrimination: A Handbook on Legal Rights for Women* Sydney: Pluto Press.

Rowbotham, Sheila (1985) 'What Do Women Want? Woman-Centred Values and the World As It Is' *Feminist Review* 20 (June).

Rubin, Gayle (1975) ' "The Traffic in Women": Notes on the "Political Economy" of Sex' in [Rapp] Reiter, Rayna ed. *Toward an Anthropology of Women* New York: Monthly Review Press.

Ruddick, Sara (1980) 'Maternal Thinking' *Feminist Studies* 6, 2 (Summer).

Ruddick, Sara (1989) *Maternal Thinking: Toward a Politics of Peace* Boston: Beacon Press.

Ryan, Edna (1988) 'Equal Pay, Comparable Worth and the Central Wage Fixing System' *Australian Feminist Studies* 6.

Ryan, Julia (1985) 'Nairobi Conference: Letter to Pamela in India' *Australian Feminist Studies* 1 (Summer).

Sawer, Marian (1984) review, Hester Eisenstein *Contemporary Feminist Thought* in *Politics: The Journal of the Australasian Political Studies Association,* 19, 2 (November).

Sawer, Marian ed. (1985) *Program for Change: Affirmative Action in Australia* Sydney: Allen & Unwin.

Sawer, Marian (1990) *Sisters in Suits: Women and Public Policy in Australia* Sydney: Allen & Unwin.

Sciolino, Elaine (1990) 'Battle Lines Are Shifting on Women in War' *The New York Times* 25 January.

Scott, Joan W. (1988) 'Deconstructing Equality-Versus-Difference: Or, the Uses of Poststructuralist Theory for Feminism' *Feminist Studies* 14.

Segal, Lynne (1987) *Is the Future Female? Troubled Thoughts on Contemporary Feminism* London: Virago.

Snitow, Ann (1985) 'The Company of Women' review Joan Kelly *Women, History and Theory* in *The Village Voice* 2 July.

Sobski, Jozefa (1985) letter *Sydney Morning Herald* 2 April; reprinted *Refractory Girl* 28 (May).

Spelman, Elizabeth (1988) *Inessential Woman: Problems of Exclusion in Feminist Thought* Boston: Beacon Press.

Statement by Hon. Barrie Unsworth, MP, Premier of New South Wales and Minister Responsible for Women's Interests to International Women's Day Reception, Sydney: New South Wales Government Printer, 1988.

Stevens, Joyce (1986) 'The Politics of Reconstructing Socialism' in David McKnight ed. *Moving Left: The Future of Socialism in Australia* Sydney and London: Pluto Press.

Stimpson, Catharine R. ed. (1981) *Women and the American City* Chicago: University of Chicago Press.

Stretton, Hugh (1989) 'Life After Dawkins (and How Australia Lost Rowley's Vaccine)' *Australian Society* October.

Summers, Anne (1975) *Damned Whores and God's Police: The Colonization of Women in Australia* Ringwood: Penguin.

Summers, Anne (1986) 'Mandarins or Missionaries: Women in the Federal Bureaucracy' in Norma Grieve and Ailsa Burns, eds *Australian Women: New Feminist Perspectives* Melbourne: Oxford University Press.

Summers, Anne (1988) 'Let Me Introduce Myself' *Ms.* January.

Sykes, Roberta (1989) *Black Majority* Hawthorn: Hudson.

Thompson, Denise (1989) 'The "Sex/Gender" Distinction: A Reconsideration' *Australian Feminist Studies* 10 (Summer).

Thorne, Barrie and Yalom, Marilyn eds (1982) *Rethinking the Family: Some Feminist Questions* New York: Longman.

Thorne, Patrick (1986) *Split* (London) 1 May.

Toffler, Alvin (1970) *Future Shock* New York: Random

Wagstaff, Rosie (1986) 'Equal Employment Opportunity, Gender and Control', Masters in Administration Thesis, Kuring-gai College of Advanced Education, unpublished (in author's possession).

Ward, Elizabeth (1984) *Father-Daughter Rape* London: Women's Press.

Watson, Sophie ed. (1990) *Playing the State: Australian Feminist Interventions* London: Verso and Sydney: Allen & Unwin.

Weedon, Chris (1987) *Feminist Practice and Poststructuralist Theory* Oxford: Basil Blackwell.

Weir, Lorna (1987) 'Women and the State: A Conference for Feminist Activists' *Feminist Review* 26 (July).

Wickenden, Dorothy (1986) 'What NOW?' *The New Republic* 5 May.

Wilenski, Peter (1977) *Directions for Change* Review of the New South Wales

Government Administration, Sydney: New South Wales Government Printer.

Wilenski, Peter (1982) *Unfinished Agenda* Review of the New South Wales Government Administration, Sydney: New South Wales Government Printer.

Wilkes, G.A. (1978) *A Dictionary of Australian Colloquialisms* Sydney: Sydney University Press.

Wittig, Monique (1971) *Les Guérillères*, tr. David LeVay, New York: Viking.

'Women in Elective Office, 1989' (1990) (fact sheet, amended), Center for the American Woman and Politics, National Information Bank on Women in Public Office, Eagleton Institute of Politics, Rutgers University.

'Women to the Fore in Norwegian Government' *Sydney Morning Herald* 16 May 1986.

Women's Advisory Council of New South Wales (1988) *A Decade of Change* Sydney: New South Wales Government Printer.

Yeatman, Anna (1988) 'Contemporary Issues for Feminism and the Politics of the State', paper presented to the National Conference on Gender Issues in Educational Administration and Policy, 28–30 November 1987 (written version, 1988).

Yeatman, Anna (1990) *Bureaucrats, Technocrats, Femocrats: Essays on the Contemporary Australian State* Sydney: Allen & Unwin.

Ziller, Alison (1980) *Affirmative Action Handbook* Sydney: New South Wales Government Printer.

Ziller, Alison (1984) 'A Legislative Program for Affirmative Action' *Equal Opportunities International*, 3, 4.

Index

language: Australian use of 8; of femocrats 37–8; non-sexist 4
La Trobe University (Melbourne) 14
lesbians 38, 87, 95; and legal reforms 22
Lewis, I.M. 109
liberalism 33, 68–70
Liberal–National coalition (NSW) 54
Lord, Sharon 23
Lorde, Audre 98
Lynch, Lesley 30
Lynd, Staughton 40
Lyotard, Jean-François 106

McAuliffe, Christa 80, 81
MacKinnon, Catharine 29, 98, 102–5, 112
Macquarie University (Sydney) 14
Main Roads, Department of (NSW) 46
Malaysia, women factory workers in 107–11
marriage: legal framework 29; power and 91; realities of 93
Marxism 98
masculinity, construction of 90
Mason, Chloe 36
'maternal thinking' 84–5
maternity leave 23
Matthews, Jill 9
migrants (immigrants), non-English-speaking 30, 34, 43, 44, 47, 71
Miller, Jean Baker 25, 79, 99
Millett, Kate 99
misogyny 89
Mitchell, Juliet 88
Money, John 111
Morgan, Robin 90
motherhood 89, 93
mothers, supporting 91

National Agenda for Women (Australia) 36, 84
National Urban Studies Association (USA) 27

Navratilova, Martina 99
New Left, the 90
New Right, the 86–7
New South Wales (Australia): and EEO programme 33–5; and EEO legislation 43–59; femocrats in 30–1; see also femocrats, and by name of government department
New York Women Against Pornography 10
Norway 75
nurses 94
nurturing 94, 95; and men 81; and women 79–80

O'Donnell, Penny 63
Office of the Director of Equal Opportunity in Public Employment see Director of Equal Opportunity in Public Employment
Office of the Status of Women, Department of the Prime Minister and Cabinet (Australia) 14, 75
Ong, Aihwa 102, 107–11, 112
Owens, Doris 35

Parsons, Talcott 99
patriarchy 32, 101
peace movement, women's 90, 92, see also Greenham Common
physical disabilities: see disabilities, people with physical
pluralism 70
policy making, women and 23, see also femocrats
politics: of the family 90–1; women in 41, 75
pornography 10–11, 22, 29, 39, 92, 103
postmodernism 63
poverty, feminisation of 76; of women 23
power: in family relations 90–1;